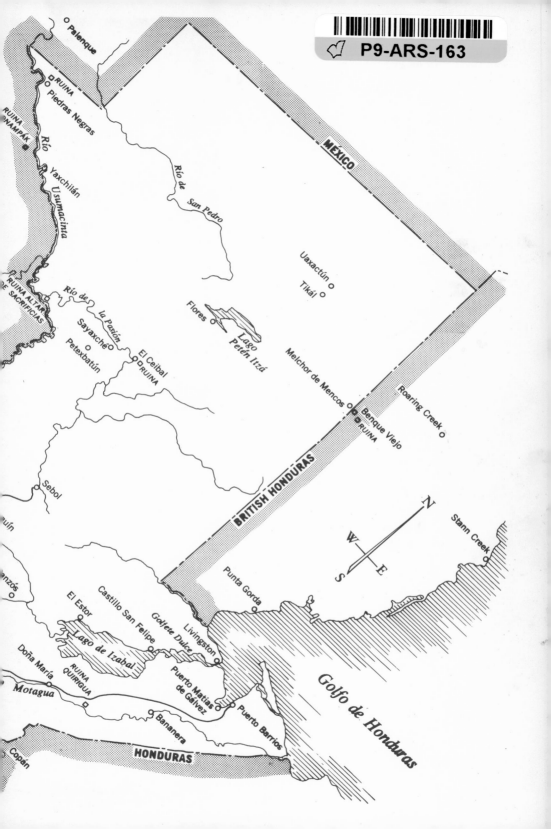

P9-ARS-163

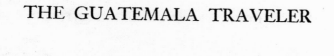

THE GUATEMALA TRAVELER

Lake Atitlán showing San Pedro Volcano as seen from Panajachel.

THE
GUATEMALA
TRAVELER

A Concise History and Guide

by SELDEN RODMAN

A Duell, Sloan and Pearce Book

MEREDITH PRESS

New York

First edition

Library of Congress Catalog Card Number: 67-11028

To

SEYMOUR LEICHMAN

who has never been in Guatemala
but who took a long look at a *rupa* from
Quezaltenango and painted
"The Earthly Paradise"

PREFACE

THERE is no up-to-date history of Guatemala in English—nor in Spanish. There is no contemporary traveler's guide. There are no readily available photographs of the most visually spectacular country on the North American continent. Belize, newly independent and Negro, which Guatemala claims and the British still subsidize, remains for most people a name on a map. This book endeavors to fill these needs; but it is charged with a more specific current.

The history of Guatemala—from pre-Columbian times when the Mayas with their genius for art and mathematics suddenly faded, through a Conquest of unparalleled brutality, to the modern period when progressive and reactionary strong men succeed one another with bewildering protestations of good faith—has been violent. Let me state at the outset that my effort to make sense of so much seeming senselessness is partisan to this degree: I believe strongly that Guatemala without fundamental economic reforms is doomed; but I believe also that no economic solution will be worth anything if democracy and the rich cultural heritage of the Indian majority are sacrificed in the process.

Let it also be said that no attempt has been made to minimize the United States' often shortsighted and sometimes perverse involvement in Latin-American affairs. But let it be recalled, too, that in 1830 no less a patriot than Simón Bolívar, at the end of his career as Liberator, concluded bitterly that Latin America was ungovernable, and that the whole area would "infallibly fall into the hands of an unbridled crowd of petty tyrants."

If I am less pessimistic, it is because events since the Second World War have demonstrated two things. The Spanish pattern of bad government by a landed oligarchy is not irreversible; and the people of Guatemala, given any chance to choose, have shown that they prefer a democratic revolution to one guided and imposed by a foreign power.

Bolívar, Humboldt, John Lloyd Stephens and other great observers of the nineteenth century were either too close to the Middle Ages or too distant from the machine to be concerned about the values of the Indian heritage. There are enclaves of native craftsmen in Mexico and Panama today, but Guatemala is the only country on our continent— and one of the few left anywhere in the world—where ordinary men and women are still arrayed like royalty and live in daily communion with the forces of nature. The fact that this makes Highland Guatemala —quite apart from its volcanoes and lakes—a great tourist attraction is secondary. Unless *enough* people, native as well as foreign, are brought to appreciate this patrimony, and eventually convince the Indians themselves that it must be saved, it will not survive our century.

Lowland Guatemala, a patrimony of a different sort and no less precious, is threatened by the same concomitants of progress: indifference, aesthetic blindness, and greed. The Pacific Slope has already been demolished for quick monetary profit. The great climax forests of the Petén and the Lake Izabál regions, with their abundance of exotic birds and beasts, face the same prospect. And the great monuments to Maya culture, which rose here and are diminished to mere curios without their jungle setting, are threatened too.

If the history, the pictures, and the travelogue that follow can serve to alert Guatemalans and friends of Guatemala to the imminence of a tragedy that would be the world's loss, they will have served their purpose.

S. R.

GUATEMALAN CHRONOLOGY

Pre-Conquest

c. 1500 B.C.   Beginnings of the pre-Classic Maya Culture.

c. 317–909 A.D. Classic Maya Culture.

c. 1200 A.D.   Peak of Maya-Toltec development in Chichén-Itzá, Yucatán (Mexico), and peripherally in Guatemala.

Conquest

1519   Cortés lands in Mexico and invests Tenochtitlán, the Aztec capital.

1524   Pedro de Alvarado enters Guatemala from Mexico and begins its subjugation.

1525   Alvarado destroys Utatlán, the Quiché-Maya capital.

1526   Alvarado destroys Iximché, the Cakchiquel capital.

1527   Alvarado establishes the (third) colonial capital at present-day Ciudad Vieja.

1541   Death of Alvarado. Establishment of the fourth colonial capital at present-day Antigua.

1697   Fall of Tayasál, the Itzá capital in the Petén and the last pre-Columbian Indian stronghold on the continent.

Independence

1773   Destruction of Antigua by earthquake.

1775   Capital moved to present site, Guatemala City.

1796   José Damas y Valle presides over embryonic states-general.

1823   Proclamation of Independence from both Spain and Mexico.

1824–35 Guatemala a state within the Confederation of United Provinces of Central America.

1842   Death of Francisco Morazán, liberal confederationist; Rafael

Carrera consolidates power of conservative landholders and church over Guatemala.

1865   Death of Rafael Carrera.

1871–85   Liberal dictatorship of Justo Rufino Barrios.

1931–44   Dictatorship of Jorge Ubico, last of the *caudillos.*

Modern Period

1945   Juan Arévalo elected president in Guatemala's first comparatively free election. Social revolution begins with the adoption of the constitution of 1945, Guatemala's fourth.

1950   Jacobo Arbenz succeeds Arévalo and two years later has drastic Agrarian Reform Law passed.

1954   Arbenz ousted; Carlos Castillo Armas takes power.

1956   Castillo Armas' constitution, Guatemala's fifth, abrogates social revolution of Arévalo-Arbenz period.

1958   Miguel Ydígoras Fuentes is elected to succeed the assassinated Castillo Armas.

1963   Enrique Peralta seizes government in *coup-d'état* to prevent possible succession of Ydígoras Fuentes by Arévalo.

1966   Julio César Méndez Montenegro elected president to succeed Peralta.

ACKNOWLEDGMENTS

WITHOUT the help of Lucy Sturgill, Guatemalan-American who was Sub-Director of the Centro Guatemalteco de Turismo in 1963–5, this book could never have been written. With her help, and that of Joe Skinner of the Hertz Agency and the officials of Aviateca, travel throughout the republic was facilitated and made enjoyable. She and David Jickling gave the manuscript close scrutiny—but neither of them is responsible for the point of view or for any errors that may, nevertheless, have subsequently crept in. Other friends and traveling companions to whom I am also most grateful include William and Rosalind Brister, Daniel Schafer, Jorge and Amparito Ibarra, George Holten, William and Joan Negron, Paulino Jarquín, Joya Hairs and Susan Miles, Efraín Recinos, William Vogt, Ambassador John Bell, Niels Halbertsma, William Dwyer, Jorge Bonifaz of the Pension Bonifaz in Quezaltenango, and Jorge Gonzales of the Guatemala Biltmore in the capital; and (above all) my wife, Carole.

CONTENTS

Part I
HISTORY

1

THE PRE-COLUMBIAN PAST

OF the great cultures that flourished in the Americas in the millennium before Columbus, that of the Mayas left most to excite the world's wonder. It thrived from the beginning of the Christian epoch until shortly before the coming of Cortés. The vast, sparsely populated Guatemalan territory known as the Petén, still only partly explored, was the Maya heartland. Successive Maya "empires" never extended further west and north than the Mexican border states of Chiapas and Yucatán or further east than Copán just across the frontier in Honduras, and all these territories save Yucatán were once a part of Guatemala. A few of the Petén's ceremonial sites spill over into the Caribbean littoral known as Belize (British Honduras), a territory that modern Guatemala claims as its own.

The Mayas in their heyday elected to live and build in the lowland jungles. Perhaps they chose this forbidding terrain as protection against predatory tribes to the north and south or perhaps from an innate passion for privacy, a characteristic of their descendants to this day. The Classic Period sites—stretching from Palenque, Yaxchilán and Bonampák in Mexican Chiapas, then across Guatemala's Petén where Piedras Negras, Uaxactún and Tikál are to be found, and finally to Quiriguá and Copán on opposite sides of the Motagua River—were so well concealed by the climax forests that still cover most of this humid region that they eluded discovery for centuries. To this day they disclose their treasures only to the eyes of the adventurous.

Somewhere in the dim, ill-defined period stretching from 1500 B.C. to 317 A.D. that archaeologists call pre-Classic,[1] the Mayas entered this

[1] Dates given in this book follow the so-called Goodman-Martinez Hernandez-Thompson Correlation, a system for reading the calendric glyphs based on clues supplied by Bishop Diego de Landa of Yucatán in the sixteenth century. A more recent system, based on radioactive carbon tests establishing the age of the wood

region or began to assume the characteristics by which we recognize them. In the Guatemalan highlands, which straddled the trade routes between Mexico and Central America and thus drew upon cultures to the north already highly developed, there was an early flowering of sculpture.

Kaminal Juyú

The site where some of the best carvings of this period are to be found is within the metropolitan district of Guatemala City, and is called Kaminal Juyú. Many of the mounds are still undisturbed, but tombs have been inadvertently revealed by bulldozers leveling the ground for housing along the road to Antigua. The finest piece from the pre-Classic, a six-foot stela dating perhaps to 500 B.C., is in the capital's Archaeological Museum. It was brought to the director of the museum at a time when smaller pieces, laid bare in the same drainage ditch, were being carried away by collectors in taxis, and it still bears the marks of the bulldozer's teeth. It shows a man with an elaborate headdress holding a baton and a hafted eccentric flint; incense burners with stylized smoke are at his feet.[2] But Kaminal Juyú, since it seems not to have participated in the Classic Maya flowering of the lowlands, has nothing to show above ground. Its early temples had fallen or been buried by the time the Spaniards came. Its late artifacts merge with the work of the Toltec conquerors from Mexico who fanned out over the highlands and intermarried with the Mayas there in the centuries immediately preceding the Conquest.

Uaxactún

The pre-Classic has been studied to best advantage in the actual Classic sites. There, beneath the great temples still standing from that period, the progression from the old to the new could be seen most dramatically. Uaxactún, eleven miles north of Tikál in Guatemala's Petén territory, is the site where "Maya time" first seemed to disclose a beginning, a middle and an end.

There are, to be sure, proponents of other regions as the "true" cradles of the Maya. The Huastec environment of Veracruz province in Mexico is one. The prehistoric Usulatán culture of eastern Salvador is another. The Miraflores period of Kaminal Juyú itself is a third. But

---

in the Maya lintels, would push all these dates back 250 years, but it is not yet accepted by many archaeologists.

[2] See Plate 1.

in the ruins of Uaxactún archaeologists found: 1. pottery and crude figurines ("Mamom" culture) antedating the Classic Mayas by a millennium; 2. a stone pyramid ("Chicanel" culture) dating from about the time of Christ; 3. the earliest of a series of stone markers (stelae) recording regular intervals of time, dated 328 A.D.; 4. polychrome pottery of the same period, more sophisticated in design and color than anything previously found in Middle America; 5. the first evidences of corbeled roof construction, a feature of all Maya architecture in the centuries to come; 6. the first astronomical observatory from which the positions of the solar equinoxes were determined; and 7. the first and (until the 1946 discovery of Bonampák in Mexico's Chiapas) the finest fresco painting of the Classic Mayas. This almost perfectly preserved mural in dominant reds and blacks was discovered during the period (1926–37) when the Carnegie Institution of Washington excavated Uaxactún; but the government of Guatemala neglected to take measures to protect it from the elements, and it soon disintegrated. Antonio Tejeda, now director of the Archaeological Museum, painted an exact copy of the two principal figures in the fresco for the museum, where it is now to be seen, and with his help the photograph reproduced as Plate 2 was taken.

Uaxactún was discovered by the great archaeologist Sylvanus Morley in 1916 on a trip that almost cost him his life. Its ruins, now undisturbed and untended for three decades, have receded into the jungle. They may be reached on Aviateca flights from the capital, but except for those interested in doing their own digging and exploring they are hardly worth visiting.

Tikál

Worth visiting for many reasons and reached by more frequent flights of the same airline at a landing strip eleven miles south of Uaxactún, is Tikál. It is the largest of all Maya ceremonial centers. Its inner core of temples, connected by causeways, covers a square mile of the semideciduous tropical dry-forest.[3] Its six central pyramids are the highest pre-Columbian structures and, until the modern skyscrapers rose, the highest buildings ever erected in the Americas. Tikál's setting, in primeval jungle alive with birds of brilliant plumage, monkeys and

[3] Sometimes called quasi-rainforest. The annual rainfall in these lowlands is between 1000 and 2000 mm. annually, but there is a prolonged dry season. None of these sites, incidentally, was a city in our sense. They were places of worship, ritual and calendric study that were the foci of the whole civilization. The masses of the people, including the builders and sculptors and perhaps even the priests, lived in thatched huts that have long since disappeared.

other animals, gives it an air of timelessness that no other accessible ruin has.[4]

Tikál's pyramids were probably built to overtop the highest cedars and sapodillas in order to study the movements of the stars. From a plane skimming over that endless sea of foliage they are an astonishing sight. But until man flew with the birds, they offered no clue to the forgotten presence of the huge ceremonial complex below. Though always known to the local descendants of the Mayas who worshiped sporadically in the ruins centuries after the civilization itself had vanished, Tikál was discovered by a Spanish Franciscan priest, Andres de Avendaño, in 1696. (Cortés, more than a century and a half before, had passed close to both Tikál and Palenque without seeing them on his fruitless march to Honduras.) Fray Avendaño had been on an expedition from the Yucatán province of Mexico to convert the Itzás. This last unconquered Maya tribe was then besieged in its island fortress, Tayasál, in Lake Petén-Itzá, soon to be overwhelmed by military power. Tikál is thirty miles north of the big lake, and Fray Avendaño stumbled upon it on his long trek home. His description of the vast ruin was perfunctory. In fact, almost two hundred years were to pass before Tikál received its name and was systematically explored by the pioneer archaeologists. In the 1880's and 1890's Maudslay and Maler spent a great deal of time in the Petén, and with their descriptions Tikál's progressive emergence into view begins.

Maudslay and Maler

A. P. Maudslay was an English antiquarian, warm-hearted and modest, but with the spirit of a scientist and the endurance of a conqueror. Accompanied by a squad of Indian porters carrying packs of plaster and old newspapers, Maudslay walked all over the Maya region making casts, collecting sculpture, taking notes and photographs for the British Museum. He came to Tikál for the first time in 1881, five years after a Swiss savant, Dr. Bernouilli, had made a furtive visit to carry away the finest of the carved wooden lintels for the museum at Basel. Maudslay came by way of Cobán, capital of Guatemala's Alta Verapaz province, and Tayasál (Flores). He was on foot, and he came again the following year. Since there are no permanent surface streams in the region, he deduced (correctly) that the Mayas caught the rain in storage basins. He himself was careful to boil and filter the stagnant rainwater in the muddy Aguada Tikál, which exists to this day, but

---

[4] An area of 576 square kilometers surrounding Tikál is a national park and game preserve, so declared in 1956, and the first such in Central America.

his Indian guides caught fever from drinking it. One of these *mozos* turned out to be a *brujo* (witch doctor) and caused him a lot of trouble until Maudslay shrewdly "offered to drink any potion he might prepare for me provided he drank half of it himself." The intrepid Englishman was also followed about the Petén by a *ladino* who begged to sell him a unicorn's horn as a cure against snakebite, claiming he had once had one from an old Negress in Belize.[5]

Teobert Maler was an Austrian who had served in Emperor Maximilian's ill-fated attempt to turn Mexico into a French colony. By the 1890's Maler had traversed most of northern Guatemala and southern Mexico afoot or in a dugout canoe. Like Maudslay he was an excellent photographer, and for a time he was employed to take pictures by Harvard's Peabody Museum. Along the way, he discovered such notable Maya ruins in Guatemala as Piedras Negras, Altar de Sacrificios, and El Seibál, becoming more eccentric and caustic the longer he lived by himself and observed the lazy, thieving ways of the *chicleros*. In Maler's view these migrant gatherers of sap from the sapodilla were already beginning to ruin the Petén. They were turning its sparse population—no more than six hundred for an area larger than the state of New Jersey—away from agriculture. They were destroying trees, setting fires, introducing new diseases. They were turning "worthless Guatemalan currency into English silver" in their greed for the quick profits promised by the nascent chewing-gum industry. "It is sometimes exceedingly difficult," the exacerbated Maler confided to his notebook, "to convince certain people that the visits of educated Europeans to the ruins have absolutely nothing to do with the search for treasure and sordid moneymaking." And then, with a note of self-pity, which anyone who has visited this awesome terrain and contemplated being lost in it will condone, he added: "Wandering about from one year's end to another in these inaccessible wildernesses in search of remnants of bygone civilizations, denying myself all joys of life, subjected to strenuous labor, many dangers, and the daily annoyances resulting from the perpetual discontent of my men,—all this constitutes a kind of immolation." [6]

Tikál: Statistics and Surmises

The Maya population in and around Tikál during the thousand-year span of its occupancy has been variously estimated from 10,000 to

[5] *A Glimpse at Guatemala*, by Anne Cary Maudslay and Alfred Percival Maudslay. J. Murray, London, 1899.
[6] *Journals of Teobert Maler*. Peabody Museum Annals, Harvard University, Cambridge, Mass., 1901.

100,000. During the pre-Classic or Formative period and in the first century or two of the Classic, sumptuous polychrome ware and stelae magnificently carved in low relief were made, but at the height of the Classic, ending with the last dated monument (Stela 11, erected in 869 A.D.) no works of art to compare with those found at Palenque, Quiriguá and Copán, seem to have been produced. Tikál is thus often referred to as a "conservative" Maya city.

Several features of its development, however, seem far from conservative. To build the three tiny, dark rooms with a combined floor space of less than 150 square feet that sits atop the 229-foot-high Temple IV, tens of thousands of men must have worked years carrying the 260,000 cubic yards of limestone rubble that supports it and more years cutting and carving steps, walls, roofcomb. Comparing this to the Olympian serenity and good taste of Palenque, the Maya archaeologist Eric Thompson has likened Tikál in its nervousness and gigantism to a Tchaikovsky symphony.[7]

Had he written following a 1965 discovery made by the University of Pennsylvania team that is presently excavating Tikál, Thompson would have clinched his apt comparison by adding another Tchaikovskian characteristic, eclecticism. For there is every indication now that Tikál was in close touch with the pre-Aztec civilization of Teotihuacán, near Mexico City, a thousand miles north. The Mayas borrowed many of Teotihuacán's decorative motives and even one of its gods, Tleloc (Chac), whose ability to bring rain was invoked in representations on plates, bowls and stelae up to 500 A.D.[8]

The archaeologists who followed Thompson and Morley also throw light on a feature of Tikál long noted with puzzlement—the apparently deliberate destruction of many of the reliefs. It is now believed that whenever a new temple was to be erected—and remember that the major activity of the Mayas was devoted to recording intervals of time, and to propitiating the sun, moon, wind and rain by carving in their honor —the old temple, whose powers perhaps ran out with the life of its particular priest, was symbolically killed. Furthermore, when the Classic stage was over and neighboring Maya tribes migrated restlessly over the whole area—as they did even as late as the early nineteenth century —each group of visitors to the complex built new tombs over the old ones, careful in every instance to include "cache items" to mollify those who had died centuries before. No wonder that theories about Tikál are constantly changing! Its remains will probably be studied and

[7] *Maya Archaeologist*, by J. Eric S. Thompson. Robert Hale, London, 1963.

[8] *Maya Mystery in Tikál*, Part II, by William R. Coe. Bulletin of the American Museum of Natural History, New York, 1965.

admired and fought over as long as men come to contemplate that inexhaustible lode.

Stephens and Catherwood

The only outstanding Classic Maya ruin in Guatemala outside the Petén is Quiriguá. Its discoverers, the English artist Frederick Catherwood and the American traveler-diplomat John Lloyd Stephens, with whom he was traveling, were romantics more akin to Maudslay in temperament than to the dour Maler.

Quiriguá is on the Motagua River in southeastern Guatemala, sixty miles from the Caribbean port of Barrios. But it is only thirty miles across the border in Honduras from Copán, which it so closely resembles. Stephens had, in fact, been studying the much larger ruins of Copán—which had been known but never adequately described before he visited them in 1845—when his English traveling companion came upon the smaller site of Quiriguá almost by accident.

Copán is most easily reached by plane from Tegucigalpa, the Honduran capital. But since it is only nine miles from the Guatemala border, it can be reached by car on Route 21 out of Chiquimula. It should be included on the itinerary of every Guatemala traveler interested in art or archaeology. Its temples and ball court are well preserved. Its Hieroglyphic Stairway is one of the pre-Columbian marvels. Its site on a riverbank is spectacular. Its sculpture, including several dozen free-standing stelae, is deeply cut in Late Classic flamboyant relief. Weathered to astonishing pinks and greens and yellows, these sculptures are equaled as art only by a very few pieces from Palenque and Quiriguá.

Stephens, hoping to save Copán from the ravages of man, time, and the river, bought the ruins for fifty dollars. How typically and admirably American is his account of this transaction! The Indians, who took no interest in the place of their ancestors, were as amazed by the two travelers' desire to see it preserved as they had been to see them brushing their teeth:

> All day [Stephens writes] I had been brooding over the title deeds of Don José Maria and, drawing my blanket around me, suggested to Mr. Catherwood "an operation" (hide your heads, ye speculators in uptown lots!) to buy Copán and remove the monuments of a bygone people from the desolate region in which they were buried, set them up in the "great commercial emporium" and found an institution to be the

nucleus of a great national museum of American antiquities! But query, Could the idols be removed?

So small a physical problem didn't cause the American to hesitate:

In plain English I asked him, What will you take for the ruins? I think he was not more surprised than if I had asked to buy his poor old wife. . . . I paid fifty dollars for Copán. There was never any difficulty about the price. I offered that sum, for which Don José Maria thought me a fool; if I had offered more, he would probably have considered me something worse.[9]

Quiriguá

Other travelers had found pre-Columbian ruins intriguing; Stephens and Catherwood were the first to appreciate them as works of art. Stephens rejected indignantly the opinion of native historians that they were the work of "savages." These stones could be compared, he realized, only with masterpieces of the Egyptian and Hellenistic cultures. Catherwood paid them his unique tribute by drawing with fidelity and warmth every detail he encountered. It was he who first visited Quiriguá, making a fine engraving of Stela E, thirty-five feet high and weighing fifty tons, the largest piece ever quarried by the Mayas. Stephens had heard that ruins lay in a huge tract of jungle, recently bought for speculation in wood by two Guatemalan brothers named Payés. Since the nearby Motagua offered a feasible means of transporting the stones by boat to the Caribbean and thence to New York, Stephens set about buying this ruin even more avidly—sight unseen. The brothers Payés had scarcely stopped to look at the sculptures cluttering up their valuable woodland, but when a note about Catherwood's find appeared in the Guatemala papers, they held out for a higher price than Stephens could afford—and Quiriguá was forgotten until Maudslay visited it forty years later.

Stephens thought that the sculptured stelae of Quiriguá were older than the smaller, more elaborate ones at Copán. Their weathered appearance and greater simplicity gave that impression. But the research of Morley [10] and others has shown them to be considerably later. Quiriguá was, in fact, a colony of Copán. It is simply that the brown sandstone at Quiriguá has proved less resistant than the volcanic andesite

[9] *Incidents of Travel in Central America, Chiapas and Yucatán*, by John Lloyd Stephens. Rutgers University Press, New Brunswick, N.J., 1949.

[10] *Guidebook to the Ruins of Quiriguá*, by Sylvanus G. Morley. Carnegie Institution of Washington, Washington, D.C., 1935.

quarried at Copán. And that the sculptors—with an exception—were less venturesome.

The exception is the creator of the zoomorphs, so described by the archaeologists because of their animal-like shapes. These huge, carved boulders seem to have been cut at a time in the Late Classic when it was no longer feasible to "mine" stelae—exactly why, no one can be sure. Size may have reached a maximum. There could have been an exhaustion of stones lying along natural cleavage planes in the quarries. The labor force may have struck.

Two of these zoomorphs—"B" and "P," erected in 780 and 795 A.D. respectively—are altogether extraordinary. "B" is a crouching mythological monster from whose mouth issues a human torso. Morley describes its inscription as "the most complex, the most intricate text in the whole range of Maya inscriptions." This was an achievement, he adds, never to be made again. But in zoomorph "P" the Quiriguans went one step further, creating perhaps on the very eve of their dissolution a work of art unequaled in Middle America.

Other Famous Maya Ruins

Maya sites, of course, are to be found in every part of Guatemala, and new ones are constantly being discovered; but the only familiar important ones not so far described are Piedras Negras and El Seibál in the Petén, Zaculeu, a mile west of Huehuetenango, and Santa Lucía Cotzumalguapa near the Pacific coast.

Piedras Negras, in the westernmost corner of the Petén, is on the Usumacinta River separating Guatemala from Mexico. It is large but untended and overgrown since its excavation in the 1930's, and the Classic sculpture for which it is famous is for the most part in the capital's Archaeological Museum. If there is a rival in quality to the Quiriguá zoomorphs, it is the wall panel Number 3 from Temple 0-13, a restoration of which is reproduced in Plate 4. Both the restoration and the original are in the museum, but the original, like most of the sculptures from Piedras Negras, was badly damaged in the violent end that seems to have overtaken this ceremonial city.

Zaculeu is not strictly speaking a Maya ruin, having been the capital of the Mam nation in the period immediately before the Conquest. By this time, and in this part of the Guatemala highlands, the Maya had already been conquered by the Toltecs from Mexico and their culture and art were badly diffused. The pyramids and other ruins were subjected to restoration by the United Fruit Company in the 1940's, with the result that the site on its clipped lawn looks rather like an assemblage of outsize bathroom fixtures. In architecture the Mams were tolerable builders in a copybook version of the style of their Maya ancestors. They knew better than to even try imitating the sophisticated sculptural realism of Piedras Negras or the baroque dynamism of Copán.

Santa Lucia Cotzumalguapa is only the name of a Pacific slope village on the main highway CA-2 between Mazatenango and Escuintla. All about it in the banana plantations, sugar fields and what's left of the jungle, lie ruined temples and carved boulders. The stone reproduced as Plate 5, from which Dale Nichols is taking a rubbing, is on a *finca* called El Baúl. Since many of the sculptured faces found in this area have the appearance of blindness, it has been surmised that the parasite filaria, carried by flies in this region only, was a plague among the Classic Mayas.

The Mayas, Then and Now

What were the pre-Columbian peoples of Guatemala really like? We have several sources of information. The architecture, the pottery, the carving, the decipherable glyphs and the painting—especially the great Classic Mayan frescoes discovered at Bonampák in 1946—tell us a good deal. A secondary source is the series of texts taken down in Spanish by scholar-priests in the early days of the Conquest from written chronicles (now lost) or verbal reports supplied by the surviving Maya peoples in Guatemala and the Yucatán Peninsula.[11] A third key, and in some

[11] In the early 1700's a Dominican priest at Chichicastenango, Fray Francisco Ximenes, discovered or was shown a manuscript chronicle of Quiché-Maya legends. It was written by an Indian who had learned to put Quiché into Spanish characters at the time of the Conquest. This was the famous *Popol Vuh*, which Morley calls "the most distinguished example of native American literature that has survived." It was brought to the attention of the world by Brasseur de Bourbourg, who published the Quiché text and his French translation of it in Paris in 1861. The story of the Creation told in this compendium of Maya, Toltec, and Quiché legends parallels in some respects the account in Genesis. (The line that appeals most to travelers is the prayer: "Grant us good roads, beautiful, level roads!")

Other sources of Maya lore are: *The Books of Chilam Balam,* a series of chronicles put together in Yucatán shortly after the Conquest, purporting to trace Maya history for 1400 consecutive years following A.D. 160; *The Annals of the Cakchiquels,* a rambling history of the legends of this post-Maya people, written at the end of the sixteenth century in the Guatemalan village of Sololá; and the less interesting Quiché document called *Title of the Lords of Totonicapán.*

Perhaps more helpful than any of these are the writings of Bishops Diego de Landa and Bartolomé de las Casas, men of genius in the early days of the Spanish colony who studied the Indians with a rare combination of emotional sympathy and scientific curiosity. Neither Landa nor Las Casas are readily available in English, but the former has been drawn upon effectively by Victor Wolfgang von Hagen (*The Ancient Sun Kingdoms of the Americas*), who presents the Mayas as people with foibles and neuroses as well as genius for mathematics and sculpture.

ways the best one, is supplied by character traits, customs, agricultural and religious practices of the living descendants of the Mayas. Certain tribes (notably the Lacandóns in Chiapas) have never been Christianized or civilized at all. Much larger groups, like the Guatemala Indians of the highlands, who have still not been assimilated into modern society, carry out the ancient rites and folkways in diluted but tenacious ways. Many of them still speak the aboriginal languages and undertake (short of human sacrifice, of course) traditional propitiations of the ancient gods.

In one of his books Eric Thompson remarks that the gods of ancient Egypt—Ra, Isis, Apis—are today no more than words in crossword puzzles; one of the great rewards of Maya research is its *continuity:* the Classic 260-day calendar of the Mayas is still used in Guatemala's highlands; sorcerers still "dice the days" for favorable omens, farming on propitious occasions only, despite efforts of church and state to stamp out heathenism. "One can never assume the obvious," Thompson says, "when dealing with the Maya who excelled in the impractical but failed in the practical."

Children of the Corn God

For a people who mined no metals and never got around to inventing the wheel, the Mayas fared remarkably well, adapting themselves to the most hostile of environments. Morley [12] speculates that they built their original cities in the lowland jungles not merely for concealment. The rich animal and plant life was a source of food. The Petén's limestone base was easily quarried with tools of stone and wood and reduced by burning, to excellent mortar. Here amid their macaws and hummingbirds, tapir and peccary—not to mention *fer-de-lance*, vampire bats and mosquitoes—the Mayas went right on doing what every Meso-American people had done at least as far back as 2500 B.C.: they cultivated corn. This was their staple food, and flying over the Petén one can see occasional clear areas—savannas—that were once presumably their farms.

Then as now, the *milpas* were planted with a seeding stick (the *xul*), and the stalks were turned over to prevent rain mold from entering the ears. In early times, weeds were pulled out by hand. Today's practice of flailing the weeds with a machete means that the bad seed is

[12] *The Ancient Maya*, by Sylvanus G. Morley. Stanford University Press, Stanford, Calif., 1946–56. This classic work and J. Eric S. Thompson's *The Rise and Fall of Maya Civilization*, University of Oklahoma Press, Norman, Okla., 1954, are the best general studies of the Mayas.

scattered and the yield of the plot greatly decreased. Since the Mayas had no way of turning the sod, they simply burned off and moved on when the harvest diminished—a practice that is ruining the Guatemalan land to this day.

To maintain a family permanently at a yield of seventeen or eighteen bushels per acre requires a minimum of seventy-two acres of land—sometimes, in highland Guatemala, as much as two hundred acres; and the *milpa* is sometimes as much as fifty miles from the home. But since corn producing requires only an average of seventy-six work days out of the year, the ancient Mayas had plenty of spare time to contribute to temple- and road-building. This leisure, in the Spanish colonial period, was employed (through various devices of legal servitude) in building churches and in growing hemp and other exportable crops for the master class. Today the Indian works seasonally on the coffee, banana, and cotton *fincas*, or, failing to find work, leaves the overpopulated corn lands and joins the unemployed—a *ladino* in dress and outlook henceforth—in the cities. Corn, in short, offers a clue to why the Indian has always been exploited.

Then, as now, the distance between a man's home and his *milpa* could be very great. But in Maya times there was nothing to make him stay away, change his clothes, and become a drifter. The ceremonial center was the focus of his aspirations. It embodied that part of his creative talent which went beyond weaving, pottery and basketwork. And it embodied—for many centuries, at least—the realization of his earthly needs as well as his hopes of survival amid the celestial hunters.

Maya Traits

Conquest and war played little part in the Maya culture. Then as now, the Indian's desire was to be left alone. Which is not to say that he was a pacifist or abhorred bloodletting. But he feuded with his near neighbors only to take slaves, and these slaves became domestics, not builders of temples. He sacrificed human life to the gods of the sun and the rain—but in moderation and more often than not by a mere token of blood from a pierced earlobe. Only two Classic sculptures, both from Piedras Negras, show human sacrifice. The Aztec holocausts of as many as 20,000 victims in a single day would have been incomprehensible and abhorrent to the Mayas. Maya hunters, Diego de Landa tells us, whispered the prayer, "I have need," before killing. There had to be an atonement for taking the life of even an animal, for death itself was regarded as defilement. (Suicide, for some reason, was an exception to this rule, being regarded as one of the sure roads to paradise.)

Maya pleasures, apparently, were more symbolic than sensual. The emphasis in the Bonampák frescoes is on music, ritual, the dance. The gorgeous panoply of the priests' feathered headgear dominates the dying warrior, the diminutive captive. Sexual continence and fasting preceded ritual. Michel Peissel describes the primitive Mayas of modern Quintana Roo as virtually sexless, copulating only in the spring.[13] Landa reported that the Mayas of Yucatán in the sixteenth century had no god of love and were "not given to erotic practices"; but they had no fiesta "in which they did not get intoxicated," and the women were expected "to get their drunken husbands home." Whether this was the pattern in Classic times as well, it is certainly the pattern today. No one who has ever spent the night at a ritual in the Guatemala highlands will forget the spectacle of the Indian women in the early morning trying to get their drunken husbands off the streets.

Morley lists other Maya traits of yesterday and today as conservatism, cleanliness, insensitivity to suffering, honesty, superstitiousness, fatalism. The Maya Indian is and always has been deeply concerned to repay obligations. He is noninventive, noncompetitive, a venerator of numbers.

The Mathematical Syndrome

Counting time still plays a part in the life of the latter-day Mayas, but it is no longer an obsession. During the Classic stage no other people then living—and that included, of course, the Romans—had gone so far in the mastery of numbers. Compared to the vigesimal system of the Mayas, the decimal one of the Romans was unwieldy. Long before Christ, the Mayas had invented and used the concept of zero. Using a dot to connote 1, a bar for 5, and various "head" glyphs for longer periods of time (one *alautun*, for example, stood for 23,040,000,000 days), they were able to compute inconceivably vast stretches of time. A stela at Quiriguá, according to Thompson, refers to a date *four hundred million years ago*.

But why? Since the object of Maya religion was to influence the elements to provide favorable crop conditions, how better could the priests retain their power over the masses than by proving that they, and they alone, understood the behavior of the heavenly bodies? No-

[13] *The Lost World of Quintana Roo*, by Michel Peissel. E. P. Dutton and Company, Inc., New York, 1964.

body, even today, can predict the *weather;* but the Maya priests, by observing the orbits of the planets in their observatories, and through their amazingly accurate calendrics, could predict such phenomena as eclipses, the average length of time required for a synodical revolution of Venus, etc. For centuries this arcane knowledge seems to have insured their dominance. The stelae were duly erected and inscribed to mark the passages of time. But then, at some point in the years 810 to 909 A.D.,[14] the whole priest-dominated civilization in the lowlands seems to have ground to a halt.

Maya Fade-Out

What caused the so-called fade-out of the Classic Mayas? No one can be sure. A key to the noncalendric glyphs—only those recording time are now decipherable—may provide the answer. For a while it was supposed that the soil became exhausted, that yellow fever set in or that conquerors from the north swept through. But Copán and Quiriguá, where the soil is inexhaustibly fertile, stopped erecting dated stelae shortly before Uaxactún and Tikál. Yellow fever is now known to have been introduced to Central America by African slaves. And there is no evidence of a conqueror's destructive swathe.[15] There is evidence, however, in the deliberate disfigurement of certain sacred images, that the priests lost face in the century of the fade-out. So until better evidence is discovered, the theory that there was an internal rebellion against the priests' authority remains the best one. Some nonconformist may simply have raised the embarrassing question: If you know so much about the stars, why can you never predict the droughts and the rains? It could have been a rebellious member of the priestly caste itself. Or it could have been an individualist, someone out of step with the centuries-old tradition of never naming a name or leaving any trace of a particular human being or meaningful event, who said one day: What have we got to lose by seeing whether we can't live by ourselves?

Not all the priests were eliminated, of course. In Yucatán, and later in the highlands of Guatemala itself, the Maya rites, melded with those of the Toltecs from Mexico, survived, alternately flourishing and decaying, until the Conquest.

[14] 550–649 A.D. by the radioactive carbon count.

[15] There is evidence of warfare along the western frontiers to the Petén, and this has led one social scientist to make a good case for a blockade of the north-south trade route—a blockade sufficient to starve out the populous lowland ceremonial centers like Tikál and cause a migration to more easily fortified highland positions. See *Sons of the Shaking Earth* by Eric Wolf, University of Chicago Press, Chicago, 1959.

2

THE SPANISH CONQUEST

WHEN Pedro de Alvarado left southern Mexico in 1524 and crossed into western Guatemala, his unwilling Indian hosts were in no condition to resist him. The descendants of the Mayas, dispersed throughout Central America by the Toltecs and other northern predators, numbered less than two million. They spoke at least thirty-five different languages, and their two largest nations, the Quichés and the Cakchiquels, had been fighting each other for decades. The Cakchiquels, hoping to destroy the Quichés, began by making common cause with the Spaniards. By the time the folly of appeasement dawned on them, it was too late, and Alvarado was able to dispose of them piecemeal, as he did the Mams, the Pipíls, the Tzutuhíls, and all the other disoriented tribes that failed to unite in time. The holocaust that followed insured that the Indians would remain isolated and subservient to the conquering race for four centuries.

Unfortunately, we have only two eyewitness accounts of this seminal event in Central America's history, one of doubtful veracity, and both extremely biased.

The doubtful one is contained in a late sixteenth century Cakchiquel manuscript found in Sololá [1] and not published until late in the nineteenth century by Daniel G. Brinton of Philadelphia. It describes in lamentable detail the intratribal rivalries that played into Alvarado's hands. How, to begin with, "coughs, nosebleeds, and illness of the bladder" struck Guatemala in 1519—importations, presumably, from the first Conquistadors, via Mexico. How Alvarado was helped by the Cakchiquels to rout the Quichés at Xelajú (Quezaltenango). How the former then persuaded him to destroy their ancient foes the Tzutuhíls at Lake

[1] See Footnote 11, Chapter 1.

17

Atitlán, the Panatacáts at Escuintla and the Pipíls in Cuzcatlán (El Salvador). How on his return to their capital Iximché late in 1525, Alvarado demanded more women and gold than the Cakchiquels were able to provide. How in consequence Iximché was burned to the ground on February 7, 1526, following which the Cakchiquel rulers, and eventually their king, died washing gold. And how finally on May 26, 1540, the latest (and last) Cakchiquel king was hanged by Alvarado, the year before the conqueror's death, "to prevent an uprising," and the "instruction in Christianity" under the Dominican fathers began.

Pedro de Alvarado

No one doubts the veracity of Alvarado's two letters of 1524 to Cortés, but no one could call them revealing. Alvarado was too busy killing to notice the landscape, and his temperament didn't incline him to analyze his motives. Consider his background—what we know of it. He was born at Badajóz in 1485, as was Cortés, and came to Santo Domingo with the other young displaced noblemen and cutthroats in 1510. From 1511 to 1518 he was with Diego Velasquez in Cuba. Even for those times, the subjugation of the Indians in Cuba was a bloody business—butchery unredeemed by either evangelism or gold-digging. In 1519, back from a short hitch with Juan de Grijalva on the latter's abortive raid along the Yucatán coast, Alvarado was off with Cortés to Mexico.

Bernal Díaz, the chronicler of the Conquest, who wrote and died in Guatemala, doesn't describe Alvarado except to say that he was blond, brave and elegantly dressed. Cortés' opinion of him may be inferred from his reaction to Alvarado's blunder at Tenochtitlán [2]—a blunder that almost cost Cortés the Conquest. If he hadn't had confidence in Alvarado, beyond his confidence in any other of his captains, Cortés would hardly have left him in charge of the Aztec emperor Moctezuma in the first place, when he went back to his ships to dispose of the insubordinate Pamfilo de Narvaez; and the fact that he didn't hang Alvarado or even demote him when he returned indicates that he never wavered in finding Alvarado's loyalty and dash indispensable.

Like George Patton, Alvarado was a field commander without peer, but like Patton he had no taste for politics or people: his one instinct was to ride roughshod over the opposition and drown all distinctions, all diplomacy, all enemy aspirations and all cries for mercy, in blood. When he panicked at Tenochtitlán and acquiesced in the senseless

---

[2] The Aztec capital, then occupying an island in a large lake of the same name; present-day Mexico City.

slaughter of the Emperor and his court, only a miracle of confusion in the Aztec hosts saved Cortés' decimated band as it retreated across the ripped-up causeways and went down to bloody defeat at Otumba. But when he had recovered from this disaster and destroyed Tenochtitlán, the brilliant Cortés, either because he was short of captains or because he recognized that almost any superstitious Spaniard would have lost his nerve amid the weeks-long drumming around the blood-spattered altars in Tenochtitlán, never hesitated to entrust Alvarado with the second stage of the Conquest.

Alvarado's two letters to his chief are much less frank than Cortés' celebrated five to Charles V.[3] In the fourth of the latter, dated 1522, Cortés had mentioned Guatemala [4] for the first time. He intended, he said, to send Alvarado south to reconnoiter with eighty horsemen and two hundred foot soldiers. Later, he had included the news that Alvarado, with a somewhat larger company than this, had gotten as far south as the isthmus of Tehuantepec. In the Fifth Letter, dated October 15, 1524, Cortés had given a very short account of Alvarado's bloody progress in Guatemala itself and of his orders to Alvarado to meet him in Honduras.[5]

Alvarado's first letter to Cortés makes plain the prejudices with which he came. At Zaputatlán (in present-day Retalhuleu province) he encountered his first natives. "I asked them what they came for," he tells Cortés, "and they told me they were collecting honey, but it was notorious that they were spies. . . ." At the crossing of the Samalá River he saw a fertile valley "covered with trees and cocoa plantations," but his only reaction to this was that it provided terrain "very favorable to

[3] *An Account of the Conquest of Guatemala in 1524,* by Pedro de Alvarado, edited by Sedley J. Mackie. The Cortés Society, New York, 1924. *Hernando Cortés: Five Letters 1519–1524.* Routledge and Kegan Paul, Ltd., London, 1928.

[4] There are several theories regarding the derivation of this name. One is that it was the Cakchiquel word for the volcano now known as Agua. Another is that it was a translation of the word for "*Quiché*" in the Nahuatl (Aztec) language. As early as 1519 peace feelers had been carried to Cortés in Mexico by Quiché ambassadors. But Alvarado, by the time he got as far south as Oaxaca in Mexico, had elected to deal with the rival Cakchiquels, to whom he sent offers of an alliance against their traditional enemies, the Quichés.

[5] By the time Cortés did arrive in Honduras, Alvarado had already taken ship for Mexico, whence he sailed for Spain to seek confirmation of his "rights" to conquer Guatemala. Cortés spent the better part of the fifth letter describing the hardships of that incredible march overland south. Passing close to Palenque, Tikál and Copán without seeing their ruins, he was the first European to penetrate the lowland jungles of Chiapas and the Petén. At Lake Petén-Itzá he had a friendly encounter with the Itzás, who were to hold out on their island-fortress, Tayasál, for almost two centuries. The disabled horse that Cortés left on the island came to be worshiped as a god, and its image was thrown into the lake during the final assault on the Itzás' stronghold in 1697.

them and not to us." During the remainder of the first letter, which is datelined Utatlán (the captured Quiché capital) Alvarado describes the ride up the Zuñíl Pass from Zaputatlán to Xelajú (Quezaltenango). He reports his defeat of the Quiché armies there, with the help of the Cakchiquels, and his determination to "burn" the Quiché chiefs in Utatlán. "Pray for us," the letter ended. "If God does not help us, nobody can."

The second letter, datelined Santiago, July 28, 1524, relates the occupation of Iximché, the Cakchiquel capital thirty miles south of Utatlán, and the campaigns against the Tzutuhíls around Atitlán, and the Pipíls, far to the southeast in what is now El Salvador.

The Defeat of the Mayas

From these accounts of the one-hundred-day conquest, and later versions of what happened as related by Bernal Díaz and Padre Bartolomé de las Casas, we may now reconstruct Alvarado's campaign and take a look at the country through which he passed.

The Pacific-slope province through which the young captain entered from Mexico is today given over to plantations of cotton and sugar cane. It was not always so. As recently as the 1930's most of the jungles still remained and coffee, cultivated on the upland slopes, had made Champerico a busy port. In a not wholly fanciful memoir of that period,[6] the German proprietor of a *finca* describes battles between anacondas and crocodiles, Maya rites around the cone of Santa Maria and the fearful explosion of that volcano in 1902 which had flung white-hot boulders into Mexico, forty miles away, and smothered the citizens of Quezaltenango in the homes to which they fled. It was during and after World War II that the jungles were cut down—part of an official disregard for the land and the people that threatens to reduce all lowland Guatemala to desert within this century.

Only the town of Zuñíl, nestling in an arm of the Salamá River below Quezaltenango, and the towering mountain slopes behind it are unspoiled. Zuñíl is one of the most beautiful places in Guatemala. From fissures in the volcanoes that surround it rises steam to mingle with the clouds wreathing the summits. Emerald-green hot springs, of which Fuentes Georginas is the most famous, are nearby. Women robed in royal purple to their ankles, their heads wound in multicolored silk *rupas*, fill their earthenware pots at the fountain facing the church. The church is golden-pink, and so is the stone bridge under which men

---

[6] *In the Land of the Quetzal Feather,* by Friedrich Morton. Devin-Adair Company, New York, 1960.

with long wooden paddles fling water on their onion and carrot patches. Every house of adobe or wood is still freshly painted, roofed with orange tiles. The high stone walls are shaded with calla lilies. Beds of watercress fill the deep gorges.

If it was so in 1524 when Alvarado's 435 warriors, followed by a scattering of Tlaxcalan mercenaries from Mexico, entered the pass, he made no mention of it. Dragging their four cannon, the heavily armored invaders would have been an easy mark had the Quichés elected to roll boulders down on them or ambush them by night. Instead, their chief, Tecúm Umán,[7] sent an advance guard of six thousand men clothed in cotton quilting, feathers and turtle carapace into the pass, signaling their approach in broad daylight with conch-shell trumpets and demonic drumming. The Indians' wooden swords were edged with volcanic glass, their javelins and arrows were tipped with stone and their blowguns fired poison darts. Against the crossbows, harquebuses, field pieces, and tempered steel of the Europeans they were helpless. The horsemen, whom the Indians took for centaurs, terrified them. And (as in Cortés' case five years before) the myth of the white-god Quetzalcoatl's vengeful return disarmed them psychologically. They were already referring to their blond adversary as Tonatiúh (The Sun).

At Olintepeque on the Rio de Sangre north of Zuñíl the decisive battle took place. Tecúm Umán was slain, his army of thirty thousand routed and Alvarado continued northeastward to Utatlán. Padre las Casas, the pro-Indian priest who came to Guatemala shortly after from Santo Domingo, summed up what followed from the Indians' point of view. Allowing for some exaggeration, especially in the matter of numbers, it is probably a fair picture:

> Alvarado and his brothers, together with others, have killed more than four or five million people in the fifteen or sixteen years from 1524 to 1540 and they continue to kill or destroy those who are left. They have destroyed or devastated a kingdom more than one-hundred leagues square, one of the happiest in the way of fertility and population in the world.
>
> It was his [Álvarado's] custom when he went to make war on some town or province to take with him as many of the Indians as he could to fight against the others, and as he led ten thousand to twenty thousand and gave them nothing to eat, he allowed them to eat the Indians they captured, and so

[7] There is no mention of this personage in the records of the time; but since Tecúm Umán has become as close to an Indian hero as modern Guatemala allows, we accept the legend.

a solemn butchery of human flesh took place in his army, where in his presence children were killed and roasted. They would kill a man only to eat his hands and feet, which were considered the best bits.

From Utatlán to Iximché

Quezaltenango, now Guatemala's second city and the western hub of the colorful Indian highlands, was only a village in 1524. But Utatlán, a deserted ruin today, was then a fortress and as much of a city as Guatemala boasted. It contained twenty-four palaces for the nobles and a palace for the ruling family, as well as the usual assemblage of pyramids, temples, ball courts and stone fortifications. With the Quiché king and his army destroyed, Alvarado made himself at home. On March 24 a child was born here to Alvarado and one of the Tlaxcalan princesses he had brought with him—the first child of mixed parentage to be born in Central America. But within a month Alvarado was on the move south and east to reduce Iximché, the stronghold of his allies, the Cakchiquels. Before he left he burned and leveled Utatlán.

The ruins may be seen today a little to the west of the provincial capital, Santa Cruz del Quiché, on the north-south road that stretches between Panajachel on Lake Atitlán and Sacapulas, passing through Chichicastenango. Alvarado described the place as excessively cold, and it still is. Pines grow along the sides of the deep *barrancos* that surround the site. Nothing remains of the splendor that must once have been Utatlán except piles of fire-blackened rubble (see Plate 7) and a pathetic little sign on one foundation saying "This is the ball court where the victorious Quichés celebrated their great victories."

According to the Cakchiquel chronicler, Alvarado entered Iximché (their capital, some miles southeast of Utatlán) peaceably on April 25, 1524. When he asked the Cakchiquels, "Who are your enemies?" they replied: "The Tzutuhíls and those of Panatacát." Accordingly, Alvarado marched against the Tzutuhíls and with a fleet of canoes attacked their lake stronghold under San Pedro volcano and destroyed it. Then he marched southeast through Escuintla and as far as the present capital of El Salvador, defeating as he went the Cakchiquels' other enemies. Then he returned to Iximché and announced that it would be his capital, renaming it La Muy Noble y Muy Leal Ciudad de Santiago de los Caballeros de Guatemala.

The Cakchiquels were not impressed. Unable to meet Alvarado's constant demands for gold and more gold, they suddenly abandoned the city and resorted to guerrilla tactics. Once more, it was too late.

On February 7, 1526, Alvarado burned the city and established a new capital, first at a place called Xepau, and later, on November 21, 1527, in the valley of Almolonga at the base of the volcano Agua, present-day Ciudad Vieja, three miles outside of Antigua. By 1528, the Cakchiquel story concludes, "all our people were extracting gold. . . . Four hundred men and four hundred women were delivered to him to wash gold. . . . Our king died while he was washing gold."

Indians and Ladinos

The ruined past . . . the timeless present . . . the desperate future . . . Iximché is as extinct as the volcanoes that surround it. Only Fuego, far to the south, still fumes impotently from time to time in reminder of the century after Alvarado when earth's banked fires rose up as if in fury against these defacers of the earth, overwhelmed their basilicas in the Valley of Almolonga, and for a while had the mastery. But Iximché, though more dramatic in this setting than Utatlán, and better preserved, is still a desolation. Its golden ruined platforms, still with traces of the frescoes that once adorned the walls, lie two miles south of the lovely colonial town of Tecpán Guatemala, halfway along the Inter-American Highway between Quezaltenango and the capital.

Atitlán, ten towering miles west, was less easily defiled. Its beauty was surely lost on Alvarado, but he could do nothing to degrade its natural grandeur or to disfigure or defrock its people. Humble them he did. To this day, the Indians of the highlands go annually through the motions of a Dance of the Conquest in which the red-wigged, mustachioed invader repeats his triumph over Tecúm Umán in revolting pantomime. But the pagan rites still dominate the imported Christian ones. The seventeen Tzutuhíl and Cakchiquel villages around the rim of blue water still defy the muted anonymity of Western dress in the gorgeous colors of their array. Behind their walls of black volcanic rock, the Indian women at their hand looms and the *cofrades* with their censers of smoking copal still hold out against Alvarado and his *ladino* progeny.

Escuintla (Hill of the Dogs), where Alvarado broke into the Pipíl kingdom, has become the *ladino* city par excellence. It lies south of the extinct volcano Agua in the hot, fabulously fertile plain that stretches to the Pacific. But no way has yet been found of translating those riches into either beauty or contentment. The highlands are desperately poor in natural resources, the lands eroded and barren, the climate forbiddingly chill; yet everything in the Indian villages is done with rhythm, poetry, and color. Escuintla, in contrast, is uniformly graceless and jerry-built. Its brawling streets are foul with flies and garbage. The air is polluted with the fumes of ancient, overcrowded buses, backing and snorting and honking impatiently. Everything that is sordid in mass culture has been imported, from the rusty advertisements for Coca-Cola and hot dogs that hang over the brothels and *cantinas* to the music that comes blasting from the jukeboxes behind swinging doors. All the symptoms of a sick society in the making are to be found in this citadel of the emergent middle class that is supposed to hold the key to progress in Guatemala: aimless discontent, the search for scapegoats (of which anti-Americanism is the most convenient), the politics of Communism.

What is a *ladino?* He may be described as a man of working or lower middle-class background who wears Western dress, especially shoes; who elects to speak Spanish only; and who calls himself a *ladino*. One who has just passed over and is afraid of being drawn back or revealing his Indian background is most aggressively *ladino*. One who has been assimilated thoroughly into industry or commerce in a big city (a secretary, say, or a hotel proprietor, or an independent businessman) does *not* consider himself a *ladino* and is therefore not one. A typical *ladino* lives in or near an Indian community, exploiting the Indian in one way or another and deriving his pleasure as well as his profit from what he considers his superior social status and un-Indian characteristics.

How did the *ladino* evolve? His evolution will be traced in the chapters that follow, but in terms of the Conquest he may be seen as the unheroic descendant of the heroic Alvarado—the man who won all the battles and lost the war, the embodiment of materialism and intolerance, without respect for life, without culture, without ideals. The failure of Alvarado and his successors to assimilate the Indian—and the Indians' failure to react to the Conquest except passively—assured a profound sense of guilt in Guatemala and the rise of the *ladino* type.

To the Death of Alvarado

The second stage of the Conquest—the belated attempt of Church and State in Spain to ameliorate the cultural vacuum and the unholy brutalism—now remains to be related. The measure of its success was symbolized in the building of the most un-Escuintla-like city in Guatemala: Antigua. But before Antigua could be built, Alvarado's career had to run its course.

In his Fifth Letter to Charles V, Cortés mentions a lieutenant of

Alvarado's who had been given a *repartimiento* of Indians to work for him and had commenced the workday by burning their chiefs at the stake. Alvarado, Cortés observed, had not succeeded in colonizing Guatemala, though he never gave the Indians a chance to combine against him. Alvarado might have accomplished the more difficult task, Cortés added significantly, had he employed "love or other means."

Fortunately for the future of the colony, Alvarado lost interest in Guatemala as soon as political decisions had to take precedence over military ones. With Iximché burned and the capital shifted to Ciudad Vieja, the Captain-General left one of his brothers in charge and sailed for Spain to answer charges of misappropriating crown funds.[8]

Alvarado's career from 1527 on may be summarized briefly. In Spain he managed to clear himself and reconfirm his claim to the conquered lands by marrying a niece of the powerful Duke of Albuquerque, Francisca de la Cueva. Back in Mexico, luck deserted Alvarado momentarily. His wife died almost as soon as they had landed, and he was jailed by the Mexican *residencia;* but Cortés, who had been absent, returned, released his old comrade-in-arms, and packed him off to Guatemala in 1530. Bored with administration there and hearing reports of the fabulous gold that Pizarro had amassed in Peru, Alvarado set sail for that country from Guatemala's Pacific shore. The Peruvian conquistadors wisely bought Alvarado off for 100,000 *castellanos* of gold,[9] and by 1535 he was back in Guatemala. Once more his old enemies in Mexico, with Cortés himself now in disgrace, ordered his arrest, and once more he set sail for Spain, this time reinstating himself in the imperial favor by marrying Beatríz de la Cueva, his first wife's sister. With her he returned to Guatemala in 1539 and almost immediately went back to the Pacific port of San José to organize an expedition to the Spice Islands.

Courage and generosity, his redeeming traits, never deserted Alvarado. Coming ashore near Acapulco to aid the governor of Guadalajara, who was having Indian trouble, the conquistador won his last battle. But as the Indians began to flee, a horse fell on Alvarado, crushing him. He directed that his armor be removed and worn by a lieutenant, lest the enemy take heart. Then, in his agony, but without complaining, he directed the last phase of the battle. "Where does your

---

[8] Charges of corruption with the Conquest in only its second decade were nothing new. Back in Mexico, a governor sent to replace Cortés had been bought off. Bernal Díaz describes some of his comrades cheating the gold content in which they made payments with copper alloys. The pattern for government in Spanish America was already established.

[9] This treasure, Alvarado discovered on his return, had been debased with silver.

lordship feel the most pain?" the great commander was asked as he lay dying. "In my soul," Pedro de Alvarado answered.[10]

The news of Alvarado's death reached Ciudad Vieja on August 29. Almost at once, as if in retribution for his sins, there began that series of natural disasters that was to destroy the new capital and later on its successor, Antigua. After nine days of ostentatious mourning, Doña Beatríz had herself named Governor and Captain-General in Alvarado's place. A three-day storm was already raging, and hardly had she signed the papers in the palace Alvarado had built for her in the mouth of one of Agua's deep gulleys, when an avalanche of water struck the city. Maya legend has it that their god, Quicab, buried in the crater, had released the flood. In any event, Alvarado's impious widow was one of six hundred colonists drowned, and a month later the Holy Sacrament was carried three miles northwest to the new Santiago (Antigua) where the Spaniards began, with grave forebodings, to build their fourth capital in less than twenty years.

Las Casas and the Dominion of the Church

Their forebodings were justified. But meanwhile an important shift was taking place in the young colony's power structure. The religious orders were beginning to dispute the dictatorial authority with which the civil-military chiefs had so far governed. As a result of the Church's victory, the Indians were saved from the extinction that had been their fate in Hispaniola and Cuba. And the new capital, in keeping with the Church's enhanced prestige, was on its way to becoming a showcase of ecclesiastical power, the most sumptuous and beautiful city in the Americas.

The change had begun in the homeland with the New Laws of 1542, proclaiming that the Indian henceforth was to be treated as a vassal of the King of Spain. Indians already enslaved by the colonists were not affected, but those still free were not to be parceled out as *encomienda* with land grants, could no longer be forced to labor and had at least vassal rights in court. The man directly responsible for this epoch-making decision was Bartolomé de las Casas.

Las Casas was a Dominican who had been converted in Hispaniola by the horrors he witnessed there in the Columbian period. The Tainos, peace-loving and generous, had offered Columbus their bounty. But soon they had been unable to pay even the reduced tribute of gold that the Spaniards levied on them in 1496. "Then straightway against

[10] *Pedro de Alvarado*, by John Eoghan Kelly. Princeton University Press, Princeton, N.J., 1932.

them," Las Casas says, "was taken the vengeance which the Christians call punishment." Some fled to the high mountains pursued by hounds. Others were captured and horribly mutilated. Thousands took cassava poison. More thousands died of disease and starvation. Of the indigenous population, estimated by some to have numbered three million, not five hundred remained by 1548. This holocaust and the worse one he witnessed in Cuba in 1511 turned Las Casas into a fanatic of the Indian cause. He told Charles V what he had seen. He wrote a devastating tract, *A Very Brief Account of the Destruction of the Indians*. And in Guatemala, to which he came shortly after the Conquest and where he was to remain (as Bishop of Chiapas) until his death, he worked tirelessly for the Indians' salvation.

In 1537 Las Casas talked the administration of Guatemala into making a pact with him. The only major tribe that Alvarado had not conquered were the fierce Rabinals, who had held off the Quichés to the south of them for centuries. They occupied what are now the provinces of Baja and Alta Verapáz. Present-day Rabinal was their capital. If the Captain-General would not permit a single armed man to enter this territory for five years, Las Casas said, he would undertake to win them over peacefully to the Cross and Crown. It was agreed. And Las Casas entered the hostile territory alone with three other unarmed Dominicans, after first having the Christian hymns translated into the native dialect. So successful was he that five years later the entire area had been converted and the Emperor ordered that its name be changed from Tierra de Guerra to Verapáz.

The Church Builds Its City

The building of Antigua was now proceeding at an evangelical pace —with forced Indian labor, to be sure.

> All trade routes led to the capital. Over them were carried the fantastic luxuries arriving on every ship from Spain. Gold, silver, and other metals from colonial mines; hardwoods and dye plants, cotton, cacao, tobacco, and other products from forests and fields; turquoise from Mexico, emeralds from Colombia, coral and pearls from the coasts. Worn by the feet of men and beasts to narrow channels that in time sank between walls head-high and in rainy seasons became beds for mountain torrents, these trade routes were doubly hazardous with hostile Indians, wild beasts, and insects—and bandits, whose numbers swelled alarmingly as more and more riches

to and from Spain toiled over the trails while the colonists' own fortunes shrank accordingly.[11]

Theoretically the native stonemasons, sculptors, silversmiths, tile-makers and other artisans were repaid by the *encomendero,* who was supposed to be responsible for their housing and food as well as their religious welfare. But whenever labor shortages became a problem, ways were found to circumvent the New Laws of 1542. The Dominicans befriended the Indians, but the other big order, the Franciscans, seemed mainly interested in mass conversions and saw no conflict of interest between Spaniards and natives, Bernal Díaz reported. Orders compelling Indians to work without pay for sixteen weeks yearly, debt servitude, and other practices surviving into modern times, made a mockery of the New Laws. But at least the Indians were permitted to preserve their culture in the highland villages, and in Antigua a lasting beauty was created by which eventually the whole nation was enriched.

Around the Royal Plaza (now called the Plaza de Armas) were grouped the cathedral, the palace of the Captains-General and the municipal government building. Construction on the cathedral began in 1543, and although it was only one of *eighty* churches, it exceeded all in magnificence, reputedly having cost 180,000 gold pesos. Its columns were sheathed in tortoise-shell. Its main altar was lacquered with gold. Its three naves had eight chapels on each side, and the ruins of some of its sixty-eight vaulted arches carved with angels and coats of arms are still to be seen framing a cup of blue sky where once rose a dome seventy feet high supporting an iron cross. The tombs of Alvarado and Doña Beatríz, Bernal Díaz del Castillo and Guatemala's first bishop, Francisco Marroquín, who built the cathedral in Ciudad Vieja as well as this one, are all here but have disappeared under successive cave-ins.

The enormous scale on which Antigua's ecclesiastical builders laid out their churches and fortress-like monasteries may be attributed in part to fear—fear of the Indians, fear of bandits, fear above all of earthquakes—and in part to a sense of security gained by emulating the princely structures of the mother country. Opulence soon became an end in itself. Life in the cloisters and gardens of Santa Clara, which occupied 225,000 square feet, has been well described as "a pleasure rather than a martyrdom." La Concepción housed more than a thousand in its heyday, including the notorious Juana de Maldonado Paz,

[11] *Four Keys to Guatemala,* by Vera Kelsey and Lilly de Jongh Osborne. Wilfred Funk, Inc., New York, 1952.

whose rich and powerful father brought on a mutiny in the order when he built her luxurious gardens and galleries of her own as a setting for her musical and literary talents and finally tried to force her appointment as Abbess. Each cell opening onto the circular floor of the convent of Las Capuchinas had its own bathroom. Another convent was famous for its cooking. A monastery described by Gage [12] was celebrated for its quarter-mile-long fishpond. Forty-four paintings set in gold, silver and precious stones recorded the life of St. Francis—of all people! Most of Antigua's treasures, of course, were either destroyed or have been removed to museums around the world; but enough have been brought back to the restored public buildings and private homes to give the contemporary visitor a fair idea of the Church's golden moment.

The Destruction of Antigua

Antigua and all it stood for was doomed from the start. But like Sodom, it did not wait to be destroyed from within: it yielded to a symbolic act of nature. There were warnings, but none of them were heeded. Fourteen earthquakes, floods and fires damaged the city before 1717. In that year three thousand buildings fell, and there was serious talk of moving the capital to another site. On October 3, 1730, a night of terror climaxed a period in which rioting, crime and famine had mingled with the fears of the Inquisition and a thousand apocalyptic cults and prophecies.

> That night in Santiago de los Caballeros was one of the craziest in the history of the human race. No one slept. Tens of thousands milled in bewilderment in the Plaza, knelt in the middle of the streets and patios, wept and shivered, and prayed in hoarse voices. Children cried and dogs yelped and squealed through the gloom. It rained intermittently. Several persons went insane.[13]

One of the fanatics, it seems, a hysteric by the name of Juana Ocana, had predicted the end of the city on October 4. When nothing happened, the people tarred and feathered her and shaved off her hair. In the black garb the Inquisition forced her to don she wandered about, subversive as ever, weeping and wailing, until finally the Governor ordered her to be cloistered permanently, where she wept herself to death. Antigua had forty-three more years to live.

[12] *Thomas Gage's Travels in the New World*, edited and with an introduction by J. Eric S. Thompson. University of Oklahoma Press, Norman, Okla., 1965.
[13] *The House in Antigua*, by Louis Adamic. Harper & Brothers, New York, 1937.

The final blow descended on July 29, 1773. At twenty minutes to four in the morning a sharp quake drove everyone into the streets. Some prayed on their knees and others sprinkled the walls with holy water from a safe distance. In consequence of this advance warning only 123 were killed, not counting those who died of fright or went mad. "The earth shuddered and waved, heaved and jerked," and almost every building save the newly completed university and La Mercéd Church collapsed. Four hundred prisoners escaped, thankful survivors removing their balls and chains. Thousands queued up to confess their sins. Thieves returned stolen property and were forgiven by their victims. Men living in sin returned to their wives. Bachelors married their mistresses. Lifelong enemies embraced. Rich Spaniards kissed the hands and faces of poor Indians whom they had been abusing and exploiting for years, begging forgiveness.

But when the Final Cataclysm failed to follow—back to normal. Even epidemics of disease, torrential rains and two more temblors failed to make the merchants contemplate forsaking their investments. It took a king's edict, in fact, to force the removal of the capital two years later to the Valley of Las Vacas, eight miles across the mountains as the crow flies. To that site, present-day Guatemala City, the citizens reluctantly repaired, by a circuitous twenty-five-mile route, carrying all their worldly wealth with them—on the backs of the Indians who had briefly been their equals.

3

INDEPENDENCE: BEFORE AND AFTER

THE resentment against the Church that came out into the open with the destruction of the churchly capital in 1773 was a major ingredient in the libertarian fervor culminating in the Independence of 1824. To understand why the liberalism that surged up then was anticlerical, why it went down to defeat with Indian backing in 1840 and was reborn in 1865, one must take a closer look at the tripartite society of colonial Guatemala.

The Church, by the middle of the seventeenth century, was supporting 840 convents and more than seven thousand churches in Spanish America. In Guatemala the Franciscan, Dominican and other brotherhoods had been given huge tracts of land and all the Indians living on them as slaves. However much this slavery may have been ameliorated by gentleness, good works and actual manumission, the agricultural and mineral wealth at the disposal of the brotherhoods was enormous—and the orders were tax-free. The Jesuits, especially, soon became an empire within an empire. And rivalry among the orders led to scandal and even bloodshed. But as the sovereign himself began to see his wealth and power threatened, he began to crack down on the orders. The Jesuits were expelled in 1767, and their property was confiscated. From this, and the destruction of Antigua six years later, the Church never quite recovered. But it remained strong enough for a century to contest the state's evolution toward an egalitarian society.

The civil administration in the new capital struggled spasmodically to free itself from the obsolete feudalisms of the Mother Church and the Mother Country. Although the Kingdom of Guatemala extended from Chiapas to Panama, the governor and captain-general appointed by the king never had the power of the viceroys in Spain's greater American colonies, Peru and Mexico. Beset by bandits, French buccaneer raids, and constant invasions from English freebooters along both Atlantic and Pacific coasts, Guatemala received little or no military assistance from Madrid. Spain, notorious for milking its colonies and paralyzing their development to protect its own shaky economy, in Guatemala's case prohibited the cultivation of mulberry trees, put embargoes on machinery needed for the sugar and indigo industries, even prohibited trade across borders. In civil affairs, the royal *audiencia* or supreme court limited the power of the captain-general. The *encomiendas*, feudal domains whose lords held those Indians not already attached to the Church in serfdom, were originally obliged to pay the government a third of their profits, but this tax was steadily reduced. "By the middle of the seventeenth century, the greatest amount of revenue came from selling public offices." [1]

The Indians, meanwhile, were consolidating inexorably their sullen isolation from whatever "the present" chose to call "progress."

The Indians: Pattern for Survival

In the 1560's the Conquistadors' chronicler, Bernal Díaz, by that time a well-heeled citizen of Antigua, looked at the Indians' situation and pronounced it good. "The Holy Gospel," he proclaimed, "is firmly planted in their hearts. Many sons of Chieftains," he added smugly, "know how to read and write." [2]

A little more than a half-century later Thomas Gage, the Protestant traveler who called himself the English-American, took a more realistic look. If Guatemala were to be invaded, he hazarded, the Indians would rise in revolt; they were not revolting now because the Spaniards prohibited them to own arms—"even bows." Their labor was being sold at "threepence apiece for a week's slavery." And he noted the pattern that was to persist into our century:

> Spaniards get Indians drunk to cheat them, and pick their pockets when in a stupor. To make drunk, rob, and occasion the poor Indians' death, those Spaniards consider merely peccadilloes, and the death of an Indian is no more regarded nor vindicated than the death of a sheep or bullock that falls into a pit.

[1] *Guatemala: A Historical Survey*, by Amy Elizabeth Jensen. Exposition Press, New York, 1955.

[2] *Bernal Díaz, Historian of the Conquest*, by Herbert Gerwin. University of Oklahoma Press, Norman, Okla., 1963.

In and out of the Church, of course, there were exceptional Spaniards who did what they could to protect the Indian against overt exploitation. The measure of their success was in the simple fact that the Indian survived. Passively, to be sure; yet with such a tenacious grip on his identity that in the mountains he retains to this day his languages, his costumes, his customs and a large part of his original beliefs. To mention only the most numerous survivors, there are some 178,000 Mams in the Huehuetenango area today; 339,000 Quichés in the region surrounding Chichicastenango and 167,000 Cakchiquels to the east; 19,000 Tzutuhíls south of this area (mostly around Lake Atitlán) and 12,000 Uspantecs to its north; and 134,000 Kekchis and 38,000 Pokonchis in Alta and Baja Verapáz provinces. These make up today, with a scattering of lesser nations, more than 50 percent of the population of Guatemala.

Very soon after the Conquest a pattern for survival was improvised. The scattered Indians were persuaded to live in villages. To these strategic locations, often on mountaintops, came the priests, inspired by Las Casas' example, to build churches, dig wells, plant shade trees and cornfields, and celebrate the newfound solidarity with fiestas and dancing. Wool and silk were Spanish importations, but to these the Indians applied their already great skill in weaving and design. Some think that the custom of giving every village its distinctive costume was a device to keep the Indians separated and easily identifiable. In any event, it persisted and led to the many-splendored variety of dress that is still Guatemala's glory.

Then as now the village bore a functional resemblance to the ceremonial sites of the Mayas. Except during festival or market days it would be curiously deserted. The men would be tending their *milpas*, gathering firewood, or peddling their produce miles away. Whole families with their worldly goods would be working on the lowland plantations for months at a time. Some would stay permanently as *colonos*, because the tillable land in the highlands was rarely more than enough to support the eldest son to whom the family's inherited wealth passed. The military and civil chiefs of the village (*commandantes, alcaldes, regidores*) would generally be *ladinos*. But it has always been the religious brotherhoods (*cofradías*), mediators between the Church and the rites, the Indian Elders (*Principales*) and the witch doctors (*shimans*), upon whose judgment the natives have relied. Against their advice *ladinos* fear to move and even Presidents have been known to retreat. Fearing the specter of Indian solidarity, the capital's officialdom has always tread lightly in the highlands. And as for the Church, fearing competition from the Protestant sects (*Evangelistas*) who refuse to compromise with paganism, it has been willing to settle for half the devotional loaf.

In the first decade of the present century, Padre Las Casas was to find a worthy successor in Padre Ildefonso Rossbach. In Chichicaste-nango this compassionate and scholarly priest, with his great collection of Maya jades and his salon at which the town's élite (from *intendente* and *commandante* to poet and musician) gathered, came as close as anyone has to giving the Indian sufficient pride in his culture to resist *ladino*-ization. In his seventies Padre Rossbach expressed his credo movingly:

> You have seen the idol on the hill? Then you saw the crosses beside it. Always the two together. That is the point. If the Indians do not forget their idols when they worship in the church, neither do they forget the cross when they worship their idols. . . . We must begin with the children. The elders live by *costumbre* [custom]. . . . I teach them that there is one God and that He is everywhere. . . . I teach them to clean their fingernails, for personal hygiene is the Indians' greatest need. . . . There will be time enough to teach them Christian doctrine after they have experienced the benefits of our civilization. I want the Indians to progress, but I want them to remain Indians, and not look up to the *ladinos* and adopt their foolish dress in return for their traditional costumes. I want them to wear a *tzut* and not a hat, but to sleep on a bed and not on the ground, which is the cause of so much sickness and the high infant mortality. In short, I want the Indians to adhere to their costumes and traditions, but to become cleanly, self-respecting, and justly proud of their race.[3]

Ruth Bunzel in her anthropological study of Chichicastenango [4] makes the point that the Indian takes no siesta—the siesta is a *ladino* or European institution. Except at fiestas he is never idle, working bareheaded in the sun through the hottest part of the day, carrying 150 pounds or more on his back as much as twenty miles a day through the mountain trails. He is honest. He drives a hard bargain only with a *ladino* or a *gringo*. He prays not for long life, or even good health, but for the ability to carry out his appointed tasks and with as little responsibility to authority as possible. "For this reason, perhaps," Ruth Bunzel says,

[3] Quoted in *Guatemala Profile*, by Addison Burbank. Coward-McCann, Inc., New York, 1939.
[4] *Chichicastenango: A Guatemalan Village*. University of Washington Press, Seattle, Wash., 1959. The field work for this study was done in 1930–32.

"it has been possible to enslave Indians without sapping their integrity, and to exploit their labor without degrading their persons." Children learn to obey their parents. "Later they obey with the same unquestioning submissiveness those to whom authority has been delegated"— the *fiscal*, the Alcalde, the Padre and on the *fincas* the *patrón*. But only in the lowlands where the *ladino* has managed to pauperize and expropriate him, has the Indian lost his soul. Here in the highlands, so long as he retains his land, he is master in his own house. To pay tribute for peace and for exemption from such dubious privileges as compulsory education is better as he sees it than to be a debt-ridden shopkeeper, dependent on patronage from above, living like a dog in sordid insecurity, without morals, without faith, without style.

Seedbed of Independence

If the Indian of yesterday and today is managing, for better or ill, to avoid civilization and its discontents, it can be readily appreciated that in the roadless feudal society of the seventeenth and eighteenth centuries he played no role at all. Under the *audiencia* of Guatemala in that period, Central America enjoyed what one historian has called "the blessings of quiescence." Independence, when it came, was a product of mismanagement, grievance, and enlightenment within the framework of the civil bureaucracy and the Church alone. Indians took no part in it and wanted none.

To the perceptive eye of an outsider, as far back as the 1650's the despotic minority was doomed, but for its corruption not its despotism. Already for a hundred years government positions had been sold to the highest bidder—their sale encouraged by the Crown. The salary of the president of the *audiencia*, Gage noted, was 12,000 ducats—"but besides this, if he be covetous, he makes by bribes and trading twice as much more, nay what he lists." The governors of the provinces were millionaires, one fattened by consolidating the gambling concessions under his own roof. "One would expect," wrote Gage with asperity, "that *some* of the offenders would be hanged, some banished, some imprisoned, some by fines impoverished." But this was not England. "Bribes took all off, so that I never knew one hanged in that city [Antigua] for the space of above eight years." That bane of good government in Latin America, the *mordida*, was already in full swing.

Gage watched the Negro slaves cutting sugar cane in the lowlands. He saw the only export crops, indigo and cacao, enriching the few without benefiting in any way the many. He saw the *regidores* dictating over municipal affairs, paying the Crown directly for the privilege of staying in their posts. The personnel of the highest governing and judicial body, he noted, was not native born. But the consequences of this static economy and political vacuum would only be seen a century later, when the winds of egalitarian revolution began to blow about the world—and then it would be too late. The destruction of Antigua in 1773 signaled nothing more fundamental than a power struggle between the oligarchies of church and state. The *audiencia* and its subsidiary officials saw in the change of site an opportunity to break the ecclesiastical tyranny. Although the Church charged that buildings were being deliberately pulled down and refused at first to obey the king's edict, the state prevailed. Church processions and fiestas were banned. The Archbishop excommunicated the Captain-General, but the Captain-General pulled weightier strings in Madrid and Rome, and in 1780 a papal bull arrived forcing the Archbishop out.

Intellectual Ferment

What made the time in Guatemala doubly ripe for change was that the emergence of a class of skeptical, university-educated intellectuals in the capital coincided with a revolutionary tide sweeping the world. In 1776 the thirteen North American colonies had announced their independence of England and their readiness to fight for self-government. In 1789 the French Revolution began, soon to degenerate into a dictatorship of the fanatics and the dispossessed, but meanwhile raising hopes for "Liberty, Equality, Fraternity" in every colony on every continent. In 1797 a Guatemalan friar, Matías de Córdova, won an essay contest in the colonial capital with a paper describing the roadless, bridgeless, bandit-infested countryside and ascribing the cause of that condition to the failure of the ruling classes to share their wealth with the working majority.

> Each Indian, Negro, mulatto, mestizo, and even the poor Spaniard [he wrote] needs nothing more than his woman. She prepares him the corn that he sows, and both inhabit a contemptible hut, denied all civility, without requiring another person to clothe or sustain them.

His conclusion, a twentieth-century historian was to remark, "constituted a lesson the significance of which Central America has not yet grasped." [5] Thirteen years later a similarly heretical priest in Mexico, Miguel Hidalgo, inspired by his reading of the philosophers of the

[5] *The Central American Republics,* by Franklin D. Parker. Oxford University Press, New York, 1964.

American and French Revolutions, touched off an armed revolt against Spain and when it met with resistance turned it into the first modern proletarian insurrection. Hidalgo was defeated and executed, but his Napoleonic antagonist, Augustín de Iturbide, not only achieved Mexico's independence but for a time was close to forcing the union of all Central America under his empire.

The Failure of Central American Union

This was the climate in which Guatemala, and indeed all Central America, now achieved independence from Spain. Spain was in no position to interfere. From Napoleon's invasion in 1808 to the return of constitutionality in 1820, the peninsula had been a battlefield; it had also been a rudderless ship swept by every political wind from Bourbon reaction to utopian socialism. By the time some stability and a degree of liberalism had been restored in 1820 most of Latin America was independent beyond recall.

As early as 1796 the ninety-six-year-old José Dámas y Valle, thirty-third president of the *audiencia*, had presided over an embryonic states-general, hoping to control the disaffection. In the wake of Hidalgo's *turbo*, uprisings took place in Nicaragua and El Salvador. Late in 1813 a conspiracy promoted by those radical clericals, the Bethlehemites, was suppressed in Guatemala City. When the news of Iturbide's independence proclamation reached Chiapas that northernmost state of the Guatemala *audiencia*, influenced by Matías de Córdova, opted for independence on its own. Almost immediately Gabino Gainza, to whom the presidency of the *audiencia* had fallen by default, proclaimed provisional independence. The declaration, drafted by José del Valle, a young journalist-patriot, was dated September 15, 1821.

Unfortunately there was no unanimity at all within the seceding states. Chiapas, and for a while Guatemala, favored union with Mexico. Nicaragua was split within itself, the liberals of León constantly warring with the legitimists of Granada. Costa Rica, embroiled with Nicaragua over rival territorial claims and already predominantly white, looked with suspicion on the racial admixtures to its north. El Salvador conceived the fantastic notion of joining the United States. This state and Honduras both feared Guatemala's domination. Panama had already left Spain to join with Greater Colombia (then including Venezuela and Ecuador).

It took two years for the congress called for in the joint declaration to even meet. By the time the National Constituent Assembly did manage to proclaim independence from both Spain and Mexico (July 1, 1823) and to draw up a constitution (November 22, 1824), battle lines were already drawn, and the Confederation of United Provinces of Central America was so hedged about with compromises as to be meaningless. The constitution abolished slavery and the special privileges of nobility and clergy (on paper) and it bravely established legislative, executive and judicial bodies to be chosen by popular vote. But it left taxation in support of federal projects to the voluntary contributions of the several states, and it proclaimed each one of the latter "free and independent in its government and interior administration." No federal capital was decided on. Suffrage was restricted to those with property. Public worship was permitted only to Roman Catholics. No army was formed. The treasury was left empty. And nothing was done to curb the rising nationalism of the five states, isolated from one another by mountains and jungles, or to give them any material stake in the larger loyalty.

The wonder is that the confederation lasted even fifteen years. Its first president, General Manuel José Arce of El Salvador, won out over José del Valle of Guatemala in a questionable election and then proceeded to alienate Liberals and Conservatives alike by favoring now one and now the other. Finally he defected from the Liberal camp completely and took the field at the head of the Conservative-clerical army—a martial occupation for which he had no talent.

The first Guatemalan chief of state independent of Spain, Juan Barrundia, was ousted by Arce in a maneuver that set a pattern for Central American government. Arce simply removed the Liberal chief of state and all other Liberals in office, replacing them with Conservatives—after a phony election. The new chief of state, Mariano de Aycinena, son of a marquis, ruled that sentence of death would be pronounced against anyone promoting the Liberal cause. But Aycinena didn't last long enough to dispose of his enemies. With civil war breaking out all over the confederation, Arce was forced to resign in 1829. His successor—and the confederation's last president—was General Francisco Morazán of Honduras, candidate of the Liberals who had just marched on Guatemala City, fired up to break the power of the Church once and for all.

Barrundia was reinstated in office by Morazán on April 13, 1829. Two years later Mariano Galvéz, another Liberal, was elected to succeed him. Galvéz went very far in limiting the powers of the Church and in reforming the judiciary and the penal code—he even established trial by jury—but his measures were carried out without popular consent and were extremely unpopular with the big majority, the Indians. Once the latter had found a leader, Galvéz and his protector Morazán were doomed.

The Rise and Fall of Morazán

Morazán was in many ways an admirable figure. To this day his memory is revered, not only in Honduras but throughout Central America—a unique distinction. Handsome, brave, and for years undefeated in the field, he was idolized by his soldiers. He was also generally believed to be motivated in his anticlericalism not by bigotry but by a genuine desire to see Central America's wealth, power and privileges more widely shared. He was finally defeated in 1838, and for two reasons. Because he insisted on thinking in Central American terms, Morazán received the undivided support of none of the five states—least of all populous Guatemala's, without which union was meaningless. The Church managed to save itself, temporarily and at Morazán's expense, because it was able to convince the Indian masses in Guatemala that Morazán was the anti-Christ and that only the illiterate Rafael Carrera, their leader, could save them from the epidemic of cholera then ravaging the highlands.

John Lloyd Stephens, the American traveler, diplomat and Maya archaeologist, met both leaders in the years when their conflict was coming to a decision. His encounter with Morazán took place when the latter was beginning to find himself abandoned by his fair-weather friends. Stephens found him unembittered. The general's first concern was for the safety of his family and friends.

A year before the people of Guatemala of both parties had implored him to come to their relief as the only man who could save them from Carrera and destruction. At that moment he added another to the countless instances of the fickleness of popular favor.... The great outcry against General Morazán was due to his hostility to the church and his forced loans. For his hostility to the church there is the justification that it is at this day a pall upon the spirit of free institutions, degrading and debasing instead of elevating the Christian character; and for forced loans constant wars may plead. His worst enemies admit that he was exemplary in his private relations, and, what they consider no small praise, that he was sanguinary. He is now fallen and in exile, probably forever, and under sentence of death if he returns. All the truckling worshippers of a rising sun are blasting his name and memory, but I verily believe, and I know I shall bring down upon me the indignation of the whole Central Party by the assertion, I

verily believe that they have driven from their shores the best
man in Central America.

Earlier, when Morazán's star was in the ascendant, Stephens put his
finger on the tragedy from the point of view of Guatemala's future.
"The soldiers marched into the plaza, stacked their arms, and shouted
'*Viva Morazán!*' In the morning the shout had been '*Viva Carrera!*'
None cried '*Viva la Patria!*'" (Much less, one might add, "*Viva la
Confederación....*)

Carrera: Liberalism's Nemesis

Stephens' descriptions of the ruffian who was to rule Guatemala for
the next twenty-five years are ambiguous. Carrera treated Stephens
well, and Stephens, always the diplomat and sensing that El Rey de
los Indios whom the Indians were already calling El Hijo de Dios
might be around for a long time, tried to be optimistic. He gently lec-
tured the promising young man on the bad image his atrocities might
create abroad and on the virtues of moderation. Carrera had already
showed his hand. When Morazán had attempted to curb the cholera
by rational means, ordering all burials to take place outside the city
limits, Carrera had showed his contempt by ordering that his own
mother be buried in the cathedral. The bishops and landowners were
backing him—what choice did they have?—but they were living in daily
fear that their uncouth savior might any day turn the Indians loose
and liquidate Spanish Guatemala totally. The shadow of race war,
Stephens makes clear, was hanging over Guatemala. Yet when the
American had his first interview with the Indian leader he gave no sign
of appreciating the speed with which Latin politics can turn a savior
into a *caudillo*.

> When I entered the room he [Carrera] was sitting at a table
> counting sixpenny and shilling pieces.... About five feet six
> inches in height with straight black hair and an Indian com-
> plexion and expression, he wore a black bombazet round-
> about jacket and pantaloons. He was without beard and he
> did not seem to be more than twenty-one years old.... It was
> hard to recognize in him the man who, less than two years
> before, had entered Guatemala [City] with a horde of wild
> Indians, proclaiming death to strangers.... An English doc-
> tor had extracted a ball from his side. His intercourse with
> all had been so satisfactory that his feelings had undergone
> an entire revulsion; he said that they were the only people

who never deceived him. He had done, too, what I consider
extraordinary: in the intervals of his hurried life he had
learned to write his name. . . .

Stephens made what was to become the classic American mistake in
dealing with dictators, right or left. Surely, he reasoned, good will is
basic to human nature, all men are democrats under the skin; hold out
the hand of friendship, appeal to their sportsmanship, reason with
them, show them the *practical* advantages of the American Way of
Life, and in no time at all . . .

> I never had the fortune to be presented to any legitimate king,
> nor to any usurper of the prerogatives of royalty except Mo-
> hammed Ali, to whom, old as he was, I gave some good ad-
> vice; it grieves me that the old lion is now shorn of his mane.
> Considering Carrera a promising young man, I told him that
> he had a long career before him and might do much good to
> his country. Laying his hand upon his heart, with a burst of
> feeling that I did not expect, he said that he was determined
> to sacrifice his life for his country. With all his faults and
> crimes, none ever accused him of duplicity or of saying what
> he did not mean; perhaps, as many self-deceiving men have
> done before him, he believed himself a patriot.
>
> I considered that he was destined to exercise an important,
> if not a controlling influence on the affairs of Central Amer-
> ica, and trusting that honorable and extended fame might
> have some effect upon his character, I told him that his name
> had already reached my country and that I had seen in our
> newspapers an account of his last entry into Guatemala, with
> praises of his moderation and his attempt to prevent atroci-
> ties. He expressed himself pleased that his name was known
> and that such mention was made of him among strangers,
> and said he was not a robber and murderer, as he was called
> by his enemies. He seemed intelligent and capable of improve-
> ment, and I told him that he ought to travel in other coun-
> tries, and particularly, from its contiguity, into mine. . . .

Although noting that Carrera's polite promise to visit El Norte was
accompanied by no clear notion of where El Norte was and that the
dictator was incapable of focusing clearly "upon anything except the
wars and Morazán," Stephens, with that characteristic combination of
optimistic naïveté and self-righteous benevolence already noted, felt
reasonably certain that his mission would bear fruit:

So young, so humble in his origin, so destitute of early advantages, with honest impulses, perhaps, but ignorant, fanatic, sanguinary, and the slave of violent passions, he wielded absolutely the physical force of the country, and that force entertained a natural hatred of the whites. I understood that I had had the good fortune to make a favorable impression. . . .

The good reporter in Stephens understood at least who was going to call the turn. Carrera "did not want money for himself, and as a matter of policy he paid the Indians but little." This suited the aristocracy—"upon whom the whole burden of raising money devolved." Carrera was already their creature, and the Church's, and a year later at Quezaltenango, when he put down a separatist revolt by lining up the city's principal men in the square and shooting them, he had shown the means by which he would carry out their will. Yet Stephens, at his last interview with the dictator, when he went to get his exit permit signed, still believed in him:

It had taken him no longer to sign than it would have done to cut off a head, and he seemed more proud of it. . . . I do believe him honest, and if he knew how and could curb his passions, he would do more good for Central America than any other man in it.

Morazán made one more attempt to unite Central America by arms, but his effort only succeeded in inflaming the separatist sentiment of the various states. On the twenty-first anniversary of independence, September 15, 1842, he was shot by a firing squad. With Guatemala under Carrera's iron hand now firmly opposed to union, more than a century would pass before the folly of political division in Central America would arouse even the first shaky steps toward a lowering of tariff barriers and a discussion of joint planning for industrialization.

Carrera's long rule in Guatemala did bear out one of Stephens' sanguine prophecies. He proved to be a personally honest despot and a surprisingly efficient administrator. When he was not warring against liberalism and protecting the privileged (whose governments in Honduras, Nicaragua and El Salvador he dominated) he built roads and encouraged agriculture. But under the constitution of 1851 the house of representatives was no more than an assembly of landowners and bishops whose sole function was to choose the president. And when in 1854 Carrera, whose powers were already absolute, was chosen president for life, even that function terminated. The Pope had decorated Carrera for his services to Catholicism. Santa Anna, Mexico's perennial dictator, had decorated him for his services to the oligarchy. When the liberals should return to power, as they were bound to upon Carrera's death, they might curb the powers of the Church once more and even to some degree that of the landowners, but they would be helpless to change the pattern by which Guatemala was now governed at home or the equally despotic *caudillismo* by which she was surrounded abroad.

Carrera died in 1865. Little is known about his handpicked successor, Vicente Cerna, except that he was close to the Jesuits and went to confession regularly once a weeek. By the time Cerna had donned his stovepipe for the second inauguration (1869), Guatemala was already in revolt. One of the leaders of the Liberals, Serapio Cruz, had been beheaded, but two others, Miguel García Granados and Justo Rufino Barrios, joined forces early in 1871 and began their march on the capital. Granados was supported with American Civil War surplus horses and guns. Barrios received arms from Mexico. In the beginning they mustered only forty-five fighting men between them, but the country was sympathetic, and by the time they rested at Patzicia to draw up a platform they had won every engagement. There was a battle at San Lucas. Guatemala City opened its gates to the victors. Granados was proclaimed Provisional President.

He was succeeded by Barrios two years later. Barrios had already made a name for himself in 1871 by rounding up several dozen of the Jesuit priests and shipping them out of the country on an American steamer. He had also expelled the Archbishop and a number of the bishops as plotters against Guatemala's sovereignty. But he did nothing to alter the nation's pattern of authoritarian rule. And failing to do so, he extinguished whatever popular hopes there may have been that liberalism and conservatism were more than slogans obscuring the persistence of Alvarado's patrimony.

Barrios: The Liberal as Dictator

On the surface it would seem that no policies could be more diametrically opposed than Carrera's and Barrios'. Carrera had confirmed the Church in its ancient wealth and power, abolishing all the anticlerical reforms of the Morazán period. Barrios revived Morazán's laws, added some of his own and carried out the whole program with more fanatical ardor. He exiled the Catholic hierarchy, outlawed tithing and religious processions, closed the monasteries and convents, prohibited the wearing of clerical habits in public, and substituted public for parochial schools. Where Carrera had ventured abroad to support conservative regimes, Barrios placed "liberal" puppets of his choice in all the capitals of Central America save Costa Rica's. The new constitution with which he replaced Carrera's seemed to be a model of enlightened statecraft—elections for judges, separation of Church and State, a unicameral legislature, a presidential term with a six-year limit, a bill of rights safeguarding every citizen at least in peacetime.

In fact, nothing substantially changed. Except, of course, for the clergy; and even there persecution had a way, as it generally does, of endearing the persecuted to the oppressed. In the eyes of the Indians, Christ's representatives began to look for the first time like the early martyrs, worthy participators in the natives' long ordeal. Since Barrios observed nothing but the forms of the new constitution, ruling entirely as he pleased, the chances for representative government and real democracy receded further into the background than under Carrera. The rule of law was demonstrably a mockery and "liberalism" could now be equated with "conservatism" since under both the landlords remained the real rulers, and the masses—Indians and *ladinos* alike—sank further into political apathy.

An American traveler of the 1880's with a conviction that in Guatemala anything less than the autocratic caprice of a Barrios would founder, reported what progress he could detect.[6] He found Barrios' appointees in the department governments to be men of character and intelligence. He noted that whereas under Carrera there had been but two newspapers, both official and "both proceeding from one pen," there were now a dozen, official and unofficial, with several dailies and weeklies in the provinces. Most admirable to his eye was the system of compulsory free education established by decree in 1879, though he admits that only 39,642 pupils out of a population of 1,278,311 were taking advantage of it, and that the budget of the Department of Public Instruction was less than a quarter that of the entirely useless War Department. He conceded that the President had "as much irresponsible power as the Czar" but excused the reign of terror to which all political oppositionists were subjected on the grounds that this is the way things are generally done "in the Southern republics."

In foreign affairs, Barrios' strong regime proved equally feckless. It is generally assumed that he imbibed his fierce anticlericalism from Mexico's Benito Juárez, who had supplied him while in exile with funds and Remington rifles. Whether Guatemala's secession of the rich Soconusco Territory to Mexico was a *quid pro quo* for this support is not clear. In a play for United States support, Barrios offered Honduras'

---

6 *Guatemala: The Land of the Quetzal*, by William T. Brigham, 1887. Reprinted in facsimile edition by University of Florida Press, Gainesville, Fla., 1965.

Bay Islands, Nicaragua's interoceanic canal rights, and (less magnanimously) Guatemala's own Ocos Bay on the Pacific as a naval station. Without delivering any of them, he did get railways, telegraph lines, and some sanitation works under way by giving generous concessions to American businessmen. On a tour of the United States he was feted by President Arthur at the White House. Lavishly entertained by the rival powers in Paris and London, he came home in 1883 to make another of his periodic unsuccessful efforts to resign and be freed of the sacrifice and burden of one-man rule.

Barrios' attempt to reunite Central America under his leadership not only failed but resulted in his death. Only Honduras supported his 1885 proclamation of unity. Liberal El Salvador, believing in confederation, rose up to a man to prevent its imposition by force. And at Chalchuapa in the first skirmish Barrios fell.

After Barrios

In the forty-five years that intervened between the benevolent dictatorships of the two colorful *caudillos,* Barrios and Ubico, nine presidents held the office. Two were repressive, and two were notably enlightened. The span opened inauspiciously with the provisional presidency of Alejandro Sinibaldi, which lasted exactly one hundred hours. His successor, Manuel Lisandro Barillas, completed an undistinguished six-year term, following which he did permit a genuine election in which the renowned reformer, Lorenzo Montúfar, was defeated. The winning candidate, José Reina Barrios, a nephew of the Liberal *caudillo,* was assassinated six years later just as he had managed to crush a popular uprising, institute a reign of terror and proclaim the illegal extension of his term of office. Until he ran afoul of the family of one of his wealthier victims, little Reinita, as he was called, had been a liberal spender of federal funds and something of a patron of the arts.

His successor, Manuel Estrada Cabrera, who ruled for two decades from 1898 on, brought Guatemala to its lowest level of corruption and indignity. The treasury was systematically looted. The Indians remained in serfdom. Education was encouraged, but only at the cost of not paying the teachers—who then forced pupils to till their farms. The last of Estrada Cabrera's three farcical elections confirmed the style of this shrewd Quezaltenango lawyer who proclaimed his inaugurations national holidays. Since military service was compulsory for all males twenty years of age to sixty, the soldiers were simply lined up in front of their barracks throughout the country. Bugles were blown and the roll was called. A campaign button was then pinned on each soldier, who was handed a ballot reading, "I hereby give my vote for the Licenciado Manuel Estrada Cabrera for the term 1917-1923." [7] Although it was a committee of medical men in the pay of the opposition Unionist Party who declared Estrada Cabrera "insane" on April 8, 1920, their conclusion was popular with the mob that overthrew him in a bloody revolt a few days later.

Carlos Herrera, a millionaire *hacendado* who was candidate of the Unionists, was swept out of office by another revolt the following year. The time was overripe for stability and good government, and by some miracle the two presidents who followed not only provided as much but assumed power in honest elections as well. General José Maria Orellano stabilized the inflated currency, paid Guatemala's debts, reformed the education, sanitation and penal services and embarked on a program of road building and school construction. He even prevailed on the United Fruit Company to sign an agreement promising to take its differences with the government henceforth to the courts, rather than "adjusting" them as heretofore through the American Legation. Orellano's successor, unfortunately, undid this promising reform to some extent by signing a twenty-five-year contract with the American banana empire exempting it from all government duties and taxes. But Lázaro Chacón did liberalize the constitution and otherwise carry on his predecessor's good works, ruling legally and honestly and greatly extending Guatemala's primitive communications system.

Sailing to New Orleans in 1930 for medical treatment, Chacón died there in April of 1931. His legal successor was Baudillo Palma, but Palma was overthrown by a coup two days after assuming the presidency; and his two provisional successors, Manuel Orellano, a cousin of the good general, and José Maria Reina Andrade, lasted very little longer in the climate of corruption into which Guatemala had relapsed. In fact it was said that Jorge Ubico, when he was elected president to succeed Reina Andrade in February of 1931, had paid Manuel Orellano, his only serious rival, $80,000 to go to Spain and stay there for the rest of his life.

Ubico: Last of the Caudillos

Last of the old-time *caudillos*, ruling from 1931 to 1944, was the picturesque Jorge Ubico. Born to wealth in an old "Spanish" family, the ambitious young army officer is said to have developed his zeal for reform while governing the Alta Verapáz in 1907. No one can deny that Ubico was a builder, a stickler for cleanliness and modernization,

[7] Jensen, *op. cit.*

and, at least in so far as his subordinates were concerned, honest. Finding the treasury empty when he took over, he ran the government on a cash basis, paying off debts and levying direct taxes to cover $500,000 worth of new roads a year, a network of bus lines, and an up-to-date airport for the capital. His Law of Probity subjected the wealth of federal public servants to periodic audit. Municipal administrations lived in fear of Ubico's unannounced descents upon their city halls accompanied by a team of accountants. City sewers were constructed, and plagues were eradicated by such other devices as obligatory premarital health certificates. Boy Scouts were enlisted to distribute toothbrushes.

The afterimage of Don Jorge—or Tata Jorge, as the paternalistic Ubico encouraged the Indians to call him—is still heroic enough to bring a tear of pride to many an elderly gentleman's eye in Guatemala. But it is so identical with that of Benito Mussolini in his prime as to suggest plagiarism. Consider the parallels. As a military figure who had never fought a battle, Ubico retained a photographer to catch him in his wide variety of full-dress uniforms—preferably on a horse. A boxer in college days, he would challenge overly ambitious subordinates to bouts in the ring. Riding one of his new roads on a motorcycle and being jolted by a rough spot, he would remove the car of the official responsible and consign him to a bicycle for a year. Riding herd over his bureaucrats, whose books he inspected minutely for evidences of fraud, he himself banked enough in excess of his modest $28,000 salary to become the nation's largest landholder. Posing as a patron of the arts, he spent millions on tasteless public buildings and monuments, including such eclectic eyesores as the capital's National Palace and Police Headquarters. Posing as a conservationist, he extended the Chiquimulilla Canal, which has contributed to the extinction of wildlife on the Pacific slope.

Carrying anti-Communism so far as to make even the use of the words *labor* and *worker* penal offenses, the Iron Dictator nevertheless set the stage for Communist agitators in the decade ahead by giving discriminatory concessions to German coffee landlords and American banana and railroad interests. (The notorious Article 17 in the United Fruit Company's new contract, giving that monopoly exemption from import duties on materials used in business and from municipal real estate taxes, was to become the most inviting target of the Marxists under succeeding regimes.)

Especially two-faced was Ubico's successful effort to endear himself to the Indian majority, whose debts he canceled. Never before had Indians been received at the National Palace—or had judgments been made in their favor in lawsuits with *ladinos*. Once, in Retalhuleu, Ubico had manifested his concern by loading coffee personally, disguised as an Indian, to catch *ladinos* evading the bag tax. American reporters [8] conscientiously described Ubico "patiently pushing the Indian along the road to personal dignity, pride of heritage, sanitation and civic spirit." Nevertheless the Indians' peonage was reconfirmed by Ubico's decree that they would have to give two weeks' free labor annually on highway construction. And the Vagrancy Law, under which all Indians were obliged to prove that they worked 150 days a year, left them defenseless before the *ladinos* whose *obligadores* sold their labor in renewed debt-bondage to the pestilential lowland *fincas*.

Retribution

Circumventing Barrios' one-term electoral law by holding "yes" and "no" plebiscites to extend his tenure, Ubico (again like his Italian contemporary) concealed a reign of terror under a glittering exterior that for a long time deceived the outside world. How many knew that *hacendados* were permitted absolute sovereignty—with firearms to enforce it—on their *haciendas?* How many had seeen the electric control board, installed in the new steel-shuttered presidential fortress by Arthur Bickford of England, to keep the dictator's own employees under surveillance? Was the National Police, ostensibly organized to "maintain public order," a private army? (Among its other duties, it enforced the "free" work on the highways.) To go barefoot in the capital or even to linger on its main thoroughfare was a misdemeanor. Disposal plants, sewage systems, and an army of street cleaners made Guatemala City from the tourists' point of view the showplace of Latin America. But during World War II, when the words of the Four Freedoms and the promises of the Atlantic Charter were ringing in men's ears, the reality could no longer be hidden behind the façade of order. *Time* magazine on May 22, 1944, commented:

> Guatemala resembles a neat well-run model prison under President Jorge Ubico, who thinks he looks like Napoleon and postures accordingly. Foreign interests find him cooperative and admire the trembling honesty of minor officials. Guatemala's atmosphere of all-pervading terror is probably the worst in Latin America.

At home, only his bureaucracy and those landlords who appreciated the low wages, open-shop policy and minimal land taxes that his rule enforced supported Ubico. A legend of the times has the dictator try-

[8] *Harper's*, Volume 185 (June–November, 1942), pp. 418–20.

ing out the loyalty of his soldiers by ordering a squad of them into a lion's cage. They emerge unscathed, but their hair has turned white; then Ubico marches in with a whip, and when *he* emerges the lion's hair has turned white. Nevertheless, on July 1, 1944, frightened by a student strike and rumors of disaffection within the army, the fearless leader turned over the reins of government to a triumvirate of officers and waited at a safe distance to see what would happen next.

Juan Frederico Ponce, the leader of Ubico's caretakers, tried desperately to hang on. He promised the Indians the coffee plantations Ubico had just taken over from the allegedly pro-Nazi Germans. He "Indianized" his secret police, though this must have terminated its secrecy. He threatened the press, acquiescing in the murder of his most outspoken critic. Finally he lost the support of the army, and in the wake of his flight to Mexico (Ubico had already flown to New Orleans), a second triumvirate of officers took over. Four months had passed. Ponce, at the airport, is reputed to have wept when a modest $16,000 was taken from him. Ubico, more sincere in his belief that Guatemala's Indians could be brought into the twentieth century by a *patron's* severity, is said to have died of a broken heart.

The three colonels, Arbenz, Toriello and Arana, who now prepared to restore order and hold elections, were united in at least one belief. Questioned as to whether the new revolution would be a success, their spokesman pointedly replied: "For the *ladinos*, yes." [9]

[9] *Saturday Evening Post*, February 10, 1945.

4

REVOLUTION AND
COUNTERREVOLUTION

IT WAS Guatemala's tragedy that no sooner was it prepared to enter the modern world—exercising for the first time the right to choose its leaders in a free election and launching the social revolution in land reform without which its peasant majority could never emerge from feudalism—than all the idealism of that upsurge was perverted into rancor and stalemate by the Cold War. The ideologies supported by Soviet Russia and the United States in their struggle for world supremacy were not so much imposed upon the Guatemalan scene as insinuated into it by native leaders incapable of solving Guatemalan problems independently.

It may be argued reasonably that Guatemala's history made the outcome inevitable; that the heritage of Spanish misrule was such that men capable of ruling peaceably in the common interest could never have emerged. But with that qualifying liability, the tragedy was no less poignant. When the free election of 1945 took place, bringing to the presidency a moderate with a program seemingly designed to bring a better life to the masses at last, resistance to change was unbelievably fierce. Guatemala was still a country in which 2 percent of the people owned 70 percent of the land. Illiterate Indians still comprised almost three quarters of the 3,800,000 population. In the capital even veteran bank clerks were drawing salaries no higher than ninety dollars a month. All the instruments of power were in the hands of a tiny minority.

Lacking industry or mineral resources, moreover, Guatemala had become—Indians with their *milpas* aside—a two-crop country. Coffee and bananas had supplanted cochineal and indigo as the money crops.

Coffee was largely in the hands of the Germans, and the growing banana business was an American monopoly. The "tiny minority" that depended on the revenues from these crops to finance the government that it controlled was doing the only thing it knew how to do: keeping things exactly as they were. Until 1945, that is. . . .

Coffee, Cobán and the Germans

Coffee, a plant indigenous to Ethiopia, was brought to the West Indies in 1723 by a French sea captain. It didn't begin to be grown in Guatemala on a large scale until the 1850's and '60's. Today it is grown in every province of Guatemala except Totonicapán, which is too high, and the Petén, which is too low; but it grows best on mountain slopes between one thousand and five thousand feet high. The predominant coffee lands therefore soon came to be the Pacific slope, from Tapachula on the Mexican border to El Salvador,[1] and the moderate highlands of Alta Verapáz north of the capital.

Under Barrios' Liberal successors, and long before Ubico, the government began to take away the coffee lands from the Indians and give it to the *ladinos*. Under a law of 1879, owners of coffee *fincas* advanced money to the Indians that the latter were forced to repay with work. So low were the wages paid that Indians rarely repaid their debts, passing them on to their children. Some of the debt-enslaved Indians remained as *colonos* on the plantations, some migrated back and forth; and since all refused to be isolated, thousands annually died of infectious epidemics unknown to the healthful highlands.

Partly because absentee owners (little more than 10 percent lived on their *fincas*) hired inefficient *ladino* managers, partly because profits were rarely plowed back into more efficient production and partly because methods and tools in this industry never change in Guatemala, all the emphasis was on exploiting the huge cheap-labor force—and keeping it cheap. Ubico, as we have seen, canceled the Indians' debts in order to win their acquiescence in his rule, but while thousands left the *rancherios* to drift into the even more demoralizing city slums, more thousands were picked up by the new Vagrancy Law and reimpressed into bondage.

By its very nature the cultivation of coffee requires a long-term investment. After picking, the beans must go through at least nine complicated operations before they are ready to be shipped. In the receiving tanks the sound berries sink. From there they are siphoned to the

[1] A one-crop country, little El Salvador is the only Central American nation that exports more coffee than Guatemala.

dispulpers where the outer red skin is removed. The sweetish slime is removed in fermenting vats. Stirred in washing canals, the light beans surface and float off. Now the beans must be spread, to sun-dry slowly, on cement platforms. They must be turned with wooden rakes and bedded away at night. Next hullers remove the parchment shell and the membrane. The bean is then polished until light blue—to impress the buyers. Fans force the light beans into chutes where they are separated and graded. Finally, before sacking, Indian women hand-pick the low-grade beans, including "elephants" and "pea-berries." No wonder the Germans, with their talent for organization and order, quickly assumed control of the coffee business! The trend had always been toward larger and larger estates. By 1900 only one twentieth of all the *fincas* were in Guatemalan hands. Enterprising Germans were cutting new plantations out of the jungle slopes south of Quezaltenango, turning Champerico, and San José further east, into the busiest Pacific ports. And Cobán, capital of the Alta Verapáz, began to look and sound more German than Heidelberg.

The Germans survived the First World War but not the second. Their clannishness was their undoing. By special agreement between the two governments every German in Guatemala had retained his German citizenship. The Nazis wooed them and they responded. When the crew of the *Emden* unfurled the swastika while on a visit to Cobán, every member of the German Club got into the picture—and was a marked man. By 1943 the United States gave up trying to keep tabs on so many potential Axis spies and got Ubico's permission to remove them to a camp in Texas. The government of Guatemala expropriated their *fincas* the following year.

Average monthly earnings on the expropriated *Fincas Nacionales* as late as 1956 were $18.18. For the Indian *colonos* nothing had substantially changed.

Bananas: The United Fruit Company

In the 1956-59 period coffee still made up 76 percent of Guatemala's export trade. Bananas, the second most valuable export, came to only 13 percent. Yet bananas, because of the near-monopoly enjoyed by the American-owned and -operated United Fruit Company, became the most inflammable political issue in the revolutionary period.

On purely rational grounds, the case against American "imperialism" is difficult to substantiate. The capital investment required to clear jungles, hold them back, plant shoots, protect them against wind and disease, and ship stems under controlled refrigeration all over the world, would have been inconceivable for government or native private enterprise. In 1906 when United Fruit received its first concession, Guatemala's richest bottomlands—centering around Tiquisate on the central Pacific slope and in the Motagua Valley from Puerto Barrios on the Caribbean to Quiriguá and beyond—were covered with virgin jungle. They produced nothing, employed no one, contributed nothing to the economy except chicle and wildcat logging.

Within little more than a generation United Fruit was the largest single private enterprise in Guatemala. It was giving employment to thousands, and at wage rates far in excess of those paid by any native-owned business. Bananera on the Motagua was shipping out more than six million stems a year by 1936. Tiquisate, abandoned in the fifties in a losing battle against the "Panama" disease and chronic blowdowns, had eighteen thousand acres under cultivation by 1939. By 1947 Guatemala was second only to Honduras in world banana production. Modern port facilities on both oceans were installed, and a hitherto primitive rail net was completed to connect them. Acre for acre, banana exports yielded to the local economies more than three times the average return from croplands as a whole and five times as much per agricultural worker employed. The earnings per acre in foreign exchange were two and a half to three times that realized on coffee shipments. The free social benefits to banana workers—in sanitation, hospitalization, housing, pensions and recreation—were unheard of in any other enterprise. For every dollar of profits withdrawn, United Fruit was leaving seven dollars in the production areas.

How, then, did it come about that United Fruit got its unsavory reputation as the most highhanded, ruthless and imperialistic of companies, known locally and throughout Latin America as *El Pulpo* (The Octopus)? How did it become the principal agency by which the needed social revolution was sidetracked and stalemated? How was it possible that as late as the mid-1960's, when Tiquisate had been abandoned and Bananera was in full decline, visitors to the shabby headquarters in Barrios and the capital who asked why the name of the company was nowhere in evidence were shown piles of rocks that were still being hurled through the windows?

The Octopus and How It Grew

In 1958 an independently financed survey [2] attempted to answer this puzzling question. Samuel Zemurray, the Bessarabian immigrant from

---

[2] *The United Fruit Company in Latin America*, by Stacy May and Galo Plaza. National Planning Association, Washington, D.C., 1958.

Selma, Alabama, whose financial genius had given United Fruit its pre-eminence, had hinted at the answer as far back as 1933. "I feel guilty about some of the things we did," he said. "All we cared about was dividends. Well, we can't do business that way today. We have learned that what's best for the countries we operate in is best for the company." The lesson was learned too late. In the days of Ubico and his predecessors it was standard operating procedure for foreign concession-seekers to bribe and even overturn by force of arms corrupt administrations that asked for "too much." *Caudillos*, willing to sell their countries' labor and resources for a price, may have been most to blame —but they were not "foreigners." The fact that the Zemurrays had long abandoned such methods by the time the Marxist agitators of the 1940's came along and made political capital out of it made no difference. United Fruit's "image" could not be lived down by penitence and good works. Not by restoring Zaculeu and making Quiriguá into a public park. Not by giving up its stock ownership in the International Railways of Central America to bury the charge that it was stockholder and preferred customer at the same time. Not even by giving its employees unprecedented social benefits.

United Fruit could point out that its wages were double those of the coffee workers', but its detractors could reply that the banana worker was producing triple the wealth. The corporation could make "gifts" to the government of tracts of reserve land, but it could not deny that the taxes it paid on its vast holdings were ridiculously low. It could rightly insist that living conditions in its clean, rent-free barracks were better than those in the thatched hut with a dirt floor from which the (hitherto unemployed) Indian had come—but who, least of all a Latin American who values his privacy, wants to live in a barracks —especially when the splendid family houses, theater, swimming pool, and golf course exclusively for the use of the (white, foreign) managerial command right next door are "off limits" to the people in the barracks? Some Guatemalans were given jobs in the white-collar echelon, but it rankled that their salaries would start below that of a new American employee with a dozen years' less experience.

The striking disparity between performance and reputation, clearly, was in United Fruit's failure to appreciate the psychology of human beings in a supersensitive, nationalistic environment or to feel responsibility for raising Guatemala's standard of living to anything like the level of the American one to which the profits and bananas effortlessly flowed. Was this United Fruit's concern? Perhaps not. But the consequences were inevitable.

The Revolution of 1945

The revolution in Guatemala may be dated from March of 1945 when the nation's fourth constitution went into effect and its twenty-ninth president, Juan José Arévalo, took office. At the time the constitution seemed mild enough, and Arévalo was neither by background nor temperament a revolutionist. But in retrospect the two events were decisive. The constitution *promised* fundamental social change. And Arévalo's disposition had been preconditioned in such a way that when it came to choosing between American and Russian influences he unhesitatingly chose the latter.

The constitution of 1945 has been correctly described as "democratically inspired and liberal in character." [3] It projected a clean break with the Ubico and pre-Ubico past where the landowners, the capital's upper class and the foreign corporations had been free to manipulate the government. Under that dispensation collective bargaining hadn't existed, and the Indians, wards of the *ladinos,* had been either victimized by forced labor drafts or left to fend for themselves. The new charter stated that "The State will orient the national economy for the benefit of the people, for the purpose of assuring to each individual a dignified existence," and it indicated that powers of expropriation and the principle of public ownership of natural resources would be used to break up the large estates. Education was to be public and universal. The press was to be free. Congress, with half of its members elected every two years, was to control the judiciary. Local government was to be in the hands of the *municipio,* without interference from Guatemala City. There were safeguards against executive misrule. The army was to be apolitical. The national university was to resume its autonomy. The Indians were to be integrated into the national system. Political parties were to be free and the ballot secret. Voting for all literate males was compulsory; for the illiterate, optional.

Spiritual Socialism

The man who polled 85 percent of the vote in a fair election to carry out this mandate seemed well suited for the assignment. Candidate of the students and professional classes whose demonstrations had toppled Ubico, Arévalo was a middle-class man of impressive physique whose lectures on education and government while in exile had stressed

[3] *Guatemala: The Land and the People,* by Nathan L. Whetten. Yale University Press, New Haven, Conn., 1961.

dignidad for the individual and the sovereign state, and what later came
to be known as spiritual socialism. This doctrine had it that man is not
to be thought of as a cog in a machine, that he must assert himself
against the regimentation of both capitalism and the various totalitarian-
isms. Material possessions alone, Arévalo emphasized, do not ensure
well-being.

Arévalo's candidacy had been opposed, of course, by the old ruling
class, partly on the pretext that he had given up his Guatemala citizenship while living in Argentina. But he had the support of the three
colonels—F. J. Arana, Jorge Toriello, and Jacobo Arbenz—who had
seized provisional power during the demise of Ubiquismo. This triumvirate let it be known in no uncertain terms that they hoped to make
the candidate their man: they removed all the nation's local mayors
and replaced them with Arévalo backers. Until it was clear that he had
the army on his side, however, Arévalo had remained in hiding in the
Mexican Embassy. Thus it was preordained that though Arévalo would
do everything in his power to carry out the sweeping mandate of the
new charter, he would not quibble over the motives of those who supported him or the means by which the new laws were to be put into
effect.

The Enigma of Arévalo

Two decades after, it is still almost impossible to separate Arévalo's
positive achievements from the shortcomings that contributed to their
undoing. Even on a question so seemingly visible to the naked eye as
the freedom of the press, there is no agreement. One historian [4] states
flatly that after one year in office "newspapers were padlocked," while
another [5] insists that "a free press was allowed to develop" and quotes
a contemporary British source as saying that "Full liberty exists, and
the Opposition newspapers sell 50,000 copies daily." The same source
goes on to say that "The social provisions of the Constitution are, after
all, not as radical as those of the New Deal in the U.S.A. or the Labour
Government in Britain." Arévalo's apologists insist, indeed, that he was
giving Guatemala real freedom for the first time in its history and
that the revolution was on its way to giving the disinherited majority
its patrimony when overthrown nine years later.

It is generally agreed that in the first four years of his administration
Arévalo did give Guatemala the framework for a modern medical aid

[4] *Guatemala: The Story of an Emergent Latin-American Democracy*, by Mario
Rosenthal. Twayne Publishers, Inc., New York, 1962.
[5] *The Central American Republics*, by Franklin D. Parker.

and social security system (Instituto Guatemalteco de Seguridad Social, IGSS), its first labor code together with unions capable of bargaining with management, and an agency (Instituto de Fomento de la Producción, INFOP) designed to plan the development of the nation's primitive, backward industries. In the absence of domestic venture capital, INFOP tried to allocate meager government funds where needed and welcomed the cooperation of private enterprise. In the labor field, hitherto a vacuum, it was hardly surprising that aggressive organizers who had had experience or training abroad came to the fore and that among them Communists, some just out of jail in the general amnesty that followed Ubico's flight, proved the ablest leaders.

In education, Arévalo the educator built schools, campaigned against illiteracy, set up an institute to study the linguistic labyrinth of the highlands, and tried to introduce the isolated Indian to modern developments without forcing the white man's ways upon him. In agrarian reform, he tried to prevent *ladinos* (though they were his principal supporters) from charging exorbitant rents to tenant farmers, and he encouraged farmers' unions to demand higher wages of *finqueros*. But he hesitated to expropriate the powerful lords of the *latifundia*, though empowered by the Constitution to do so when in the public interest.

Between 1946 and 1950 the Office of Foreign Agricultural Relations received more dollar assistance from the United States than any Latin American country was receiving, but since most of it went to big business rather than to the emerging middle class that was backing the revolution, nothing was done to counter the rising chorus of the Leftists' anti-*gringo* propaganda—a successful search for a scapegoat to which the increasingly frustrated Arévalo was already turning.

Communist Infiltration Begins

The President's frustration in the political arena had been manifest as early as April of 1945 when the first of many plots against him was discovered. All the defeated presidential candidates were immediately rounded up and deported, although this was expressly prohibited by the constitution.

Toward the Communists Arévalo's policy was ambiguous. When they had captured the leadership of the federation formed from the two parties that had elected him, he frowned, forcing the creation of an independent organization—which the Communists promptly captured in turn. He did close a school for Communist indoctrination supported by the unions. But on the other hand the Chilean Communist Deputy César Godoy Urrutia had been his guest at the inauguration. He had welcomed to Guatemala such leaders of the Communist movement as Lombardo Toledano of Mexico, Giuseppe Vittorio of Italy, José Zamora of El Salvador, Blas Roca of Cuba, and Pablo Neruda of Chile. The labor leaders strengthened the hand of the native Marxists in the unions. The poet worked on the intellectuals. Another Chilean Communist, Virginia Bravoatelier, was made head of rural education. Fronts like the Vanguardia Democrática were established to catch those in between. Arévalo's answer to charges that he was being "soft" was that he would not have Guatemala's freedom of action strangled by the fears and prejudices of North America.

The turning point—the point at which Arévalo lost his own freedom of choice—came in 1949 when his chief of the armed forces, Francisco Javier Arana, was assassinated. All three members of the preceding military triumvirate had been included in Arévalo's cabinet, but Arana had announced his intentions of running for the presidency in 1950; and he was believed to have the backing of the rightist Partido de Unificación Anticomunista. This organization, which hoped to return the landlords to power and restore authority to the Church, had profited the year before by strikes against the United Fruit Company; these the American corporation had countered by shutting down its Tiquisate plantations for a day and defying a government order to arbitrate at Bananera. The corporation had even been so ill-advised as to take its case before the United States Congress in Washington, where Senator Lodge had characterized President Arévalo as "Communistically inclined." [6] By siding with reaction and encouraging a private business corporation to defy a sovereign government, United States policymakers (Arévalo apologists claim) thus forced the "moderate" Arévalo to take the Communist line, for had he given in to the *Frutera* and broken the unions he would have been a traitor to Guatemala.

The case for Arévalo as a disinterested liberal reformer was not strengthened, however, by his acquiescence in Arana's murder, or by his subsequent support for those who rode to power as a consequence of the crime. Colonel Arana was lured to Lake Amatitlán on the pretext that an arms cache had been found. There his weapons carrier was ambushed, and he was gunned down with his party. One of the ambushers turned out to be the chauffeur of Colonel Arbenz, the defense minister, and all the evidence pointed to Arbenz as instigator of the plot. Though he had not yet definitely signified that he would run for the presidency against Arana, it was known that Arbenz' candidacy

---

[6] *Organized Labor in Guatemala 1944–49*, by Archer C. Bush, as quoted in *Central America* by Mario Rodriguez. Prentice-Hall, Inc., Englewood Cliffs, N. J., 1965.

had the support of the now all-powerful unions—and of the Communists who by this time controlled them. Arévalo, either from fear of Arbenz and the army or because he wanted the revolution to keep its momentum at any cost, made no investigation into the assassination and spent the remainder of his term warding off the redoubled efforts of the right to unseat him. One of these efforts was an unsuccessful assault on an air base, led by Colonel Carlos Castillo Armas, who escaped thereafter from prison to fight again.

It remains to be said that despite this sorry conclusion to his presidency and regardless of his subsequent career in exile as a writer of fraudulent anti-American polemics, Arévalo's place in Guatemala's history is secure. He was the spokesman for social changes centuries overdue and their instigator. A more courageous, less vindictive, wiser man might have accomplished what Arévalo sought to bring about. Whether it was too late then or is too late now to bring about fundamental changes in Guatemala by democratic means no man can know. But most ordinary citizens of Guatemala today, *ladino* or Indian, understand what Arévalo tried to do and when asked whom they consider Guatemala's best president almost invariably shake their heads sadly and answer "Arévalo." Very few of them have been heard to say "Arbenz."

Arbenz' Swing to the Left

Jacobo Arbenz Guzmán was the son of a German-Swiss druggist of Quezaltenango and a *ladino* mother. The father had committed suicide, leaving his son to be brought up in the Escuela Politécnica, where he stayed on to become instructor and director. In the army his fellow officers feared Arbenz as a perfectionist and disciplinarian. His reputation for ruthlessness was enhanced by an introvert personality. He delivered orders almost in a whisper from behind a visage as forbidding as Himmler's, and his motives were always shrouded in secrecy. In private life, as he clawed his way to wealth and power, fierce resentments smoldered behind Arbenz' expressionless façade. As a member of the money-hungry, status-seeking *chivos* of Quezaltenango, the aristocracy of the capital would have nothing to do with him. When he married a coffee heiress from Salvadorean society, her family disinherited her. For a while she tinted photographs at one dollar a day to supplement her husband's sixty-dollars-a-month lieutenant's pay, and in her bitterness she turned to Marxism. The Communists could not have asked for a more perfect instrument than Arbenz, yet even their foremost intellectual found him hard to take. The poet Luis Cardozo y Aragón was later to describe Arbenz as "a professional soldier, who from the petit bourgeoisie rose to become a great landowner and a member of the great cotton-growing bourgeoisie; a sour man who had not ripened, filled with good intentions. . . ."

With the soul of a *ladino* and the arrogance of the Master Race, Arbenz didn't have to be told that destiny had marked him to be the Indians' *patrón,* commissar and savior. Arévalo's moderate Law of Forced Rental had not worked—except to destroy friendly relations between sharecroppers and small farmers. The big holdings remained intact, many of them vacant.

The Agrarian Reform Law

In 1952 Arbenz rammed through Congress an Agrarian Reform Law that provided for expropriation of lands not under cultivation and for parceling out of government lands (such as the Cobán coffee *fincas* taken from the Germans) to landless workers. Once more, as under Arévalo, the government seemed to be asking for no more than what was long overdue in terms of social justice and economic sanity. But again—only now far more so—the methods used to carry out the revolution gave every indication of a political power play. The landless were barraged with propaganda urging them to *demand* the land and to seize it if necessary. American corporations, and especially the United Fruit Company, were made the whipping-boys for the program's every failure.

Nor were the landless satisfied. Only the lands of the national *fincas* were distributed. And Arbenz made the disastrous mistake of leasing even those lands on a lifetime-use basis (*usufructo vitalicio*) rather than giving them outright, with the result that the dispossessed acquired no real stake in Guatemala—or in Arbenz' brand of communism. A clause in the law granting to *colonos* on the *fincas* the garden plots and houses they lived in (thus penalizing most of those landlords who were actually helping their workers), aroused such understandable fury that some plantation owners went so far as to burn the shacks of the workers so there would be no community to expropriate. In all disputes, the law declared, the president's word was to be final, without recourse to the courts.

Dictatorship of the Left was now a fact. The Communists had not taken over the government; they had no reason to. The hysterical Arbenz was already mouthing their stock international deceits (including such farfetched ones as the charge that the United States was using bacteriological warfare in Korea) and on the home front he was setting the stage for civil war, the *sine qua non* of all Communist takeovers. There remained only one detail. To ensure that the civil war be *won*, the support of the army would have to be guaranteed or the Communist-led unions would have to arm their own members.

This highly important detail Arbenz had overlooked—until it was too late. On February 5, 1953, the Supreme Court had voted 5 to 4 to hear an appeal against expropriation under the Agrarian Law. That night Congress was convened. With its First Secretary, a Communist deputy,[7] taking charge, the five judges who had voted to hear the appeal were dismissed. Between that date and April of 1954 thirty estates were taken over illegally by armed laborers. The following month Guatemalan agents instituted a strike against United Fruit across the border from Puerto Barrios in Honduras, and the government of Honduras charged that Communist infiltration was taking place on a large scale. Colonel Castillo Armas, meanwhile, had gone to Honduras to begin recruiting Guatemalan exiles there for an Army of Liberation.

Counterrevolution: How and by Whom

The die was cast when on May 15 a Swedish freighter that had loaded in Communist Poland what was supposed to be a cargo of agricultural machinery unloaded at Barrios over four million pounds of Czechoslovak weapons, a cargo that filled 119 freight cars. A few days later it was announced that an armed militia was being formed.

In the first week of June the Guatemalan Army, evidently in fear that it was about to lose its power, demanded that Arbenz publicly disassociate himself from Communism. Arbenz refused. On June 18 Castillo Armas with three hundred poorly equipped soldiers crossed the Honduran frontier but stalled six miles inside Guatemala at Esquipulas, the town famous for its shrine of the Black Christ. In the week that followed three small planes, presumably piloted by Americans in the pay of the Central Intelligence Agency, bombed the capital from time to time. A P-47 piloted by the freebooter Jerry Delarm blew up a part of the government's oil reserve. No one was killed during these raids, but apparently Arbenz felt that his regime was doomed. The same message was conveyed to the President by the American Ambassador, John

[7] Victor Manuel Gutiérrez, who then headed one of Guatemala's two Communist parties. José Manuel Fortuny headed the other. Both parties had come into the open in 1950. Between them they controlled the confederations of labor and farm workers. Gutiérrez was in line to succeed Arbenz should the president die in office.

Peurifoy, who was in touch with the two principal Guatemalans in opposition. One of these, of course, was Castillo Armas. The other was General Miguel Ydígoras Fuentes, who had lost the election of 1950 to Arbenz (by fraud, he claimed), and who was currently shuttling back and forth between Nicaragua, Costa Rica and El Salvador, waiting for Arbenz' overthrow.

On June 25 Arbenz ordered the chief of staff of the armed forces to arm the peoples' militia and crush the stalled invaders. The army said flatly No. Two days later, at the suggestion of the chief of staff, Arbenz resigned. A few days later he, and most of the top Communists in the country,[8] who had taken refuge in the various Latin American embassies, were flown out of the country, and Castillo Armas was in power.

What had happened? Communists, anti-Americans, and many liberals throughout the hemisphere were quick to charge that Arbenz was the victim of American power. Few would deny that the United Fruit Company had cried for help. Few would deny that Washington wanted Arbenz out—though less to comfort business in distress than to prevent the installation of a Soviet base within an hour's flight of the Canal. Few would deny that Peurifoy had maneuvered tirelessly, or that the CIA had done what it could to harass Arbenz with its agents and its money. Few would deny that the landowners and businessmen of Guatemala had done everything in their limited power to bring their enemy down. Money and arms for the Dominican dictator Trujillo, it has been alleged, played a part.

Yet none of these forces or even their combination would have been enough to topple Arbenz. Arbenz had fallen for three reasons: 1. At the moment of truth, when he might have rallied the masses to save their revolution, Arbenz thought only of saving himself. 2. The army, fearing to be superseded by the armed militia, refused to issue bolt actions to rifles and would not make the minimal thrust required to overwhelm Castillo Armas' ragged band. 3. And perhaps most important, Arbenz by 1954 had lost the confidence and respect of the Guatemalan people.

Castillo Armas

It was for these reasons, and certainly not because he threatened to reverse the revolution and restore the old order, that Castillo Armas

---

[8] Including the Argentinian Ernesto "Che" Guevara, soon to win fame and success in Cuba and then to drop out of sight.

was welcomed into the capital as a conquering hero. Everyone knew that he was a brave man, who had tunneled his way out of Arbenz' prison to fight against great odds for what he believed to be right. Had not this respect for Castillo Armas' courage and integrity been almost universal, he could never have done what he did. For he did undo the revolution—or most of it—within the three years preceding his assassination. The very first act of his junta was to cancel the rights of the illiterates to vote, thus disenfranchising at a stroke more than half the population, the Indians. Within a month after being confirmed in the presidency (by an Ubico-like plebiscite) he abolished the constitution by decree, banned all parties left of center, declared his opponents Communists with no right of appeal, restored its holdings to the United Fruit Company, and returned to the landlords 800,000 acres of land that had been distributed to the peasants. "Everything that led to Arbenz' takeover was as it had been before." [9] But was it?

The assassination of Castillo Armas that took place, in the presence of his wife, on July 26, 1957, has never been satisfactorily explained. The member of his guard, Romeo Vasquez Sanchez, who shot him and later committed suicide, has been called a Communist agent. While serving as a young soldier in Retalhuleu, he had written a letter to the Voice of Moscow radio asking how he might help restore the revolution. This much is known. The letter was intercepted. How he received employment six months later in the palace guard is a mystery. If he did make contact with the Communists during those six months and carry out the crime at their instigation, there is no proof of it. There are just as many advocates of the theory that Castillo Armas was shot at the instigation of his party's conservatives (or of Trujillo), infuriated by the gibes of the liberal Foreign Minister, Jorge Skinner Klee.

It was a fact that the new constitution of 1956 (Guatemala's fifth) did recognize the basic freedoms and social obligations, though less specifically (and less discriminatorily) than Arévalo's. Labor unions, provided they purged themselves of Communists, were recognized. Arévalo's social security and development agencies, IGSS and INFOP, survived. Even agrarian reform continued in a mild way, and when Castillo Armas did parcel out government lands to needy peasants (which he did from time to time) he didn't make Arbenz' mistake of giving on a lend-lease basis. The great Atlantic Highway from Guatemala City to Puerto Barrios that Arbenz had begun, to put "United Fruit's railway" out of business, Castillo Armas finished, and finished

[9] *The Invisible Government,* by David Wise and Thomas B. Ross. Random House, Inc., New York, 1964.

well. But perhaps the most important of the Little Colonel's achievements was a negative one, one that would wait for a long time after his death to be realized. He gave Guatemala a second chance to achieve a social revolution without totalitarian interference: a chance to become a democracy.

5

GUATEMALA TODAY

THE personality of Miguel Ydígoras Fuentes, the old general who assumed Castillo Armas' mantle in 1958 and ruled Guatemala until overthrown in 1963 by his defense minister, Colonel Enrique Peralta Azurdia, is more interesting than anything accomplished during those five years of bumbling.

Ydígoras did all the wrong things, but no one ever accused him of not having his heart in the right place. Or of being a hypocrite. When demands were made that a Spanish journalist be expelled for calling Guatemala "a country of Indians and half-breeds," Ydígoras remarked mildly, "I am a half-breed myself." He was fat, lusty, a great laugher, and he had the capacity of making his critics laugh with him—at least for a while. Mario Rosenthal, his staunchest defender,[1] tells of a breakfast at which the President's secretary of the treasury was being hotly accused of withholding funds earmarked for the Spring Fair. Ydígoras responded with a story. It seems that a village priest asked his Indian sexton to ring the church bells three times—"The first to awaken me, the second to awaken the parishioners, the third to call them to Mass." When the bells never rang at all, the priest asked the sexton why, and the latter replied: "Three excellent reasons. In the first place, there are no bells...." The priest didn't inquire about the other two reasons. And Ydígoras' critics emulated the priest.

The fact that the anecdote evaded the facts is perhaps the point. When criticized more harshly for corruption in his official family, Ydígoras brought his whole cabinet before the television cameras and asked each secretary, "Have you personally stolen anything?" Their indignant Nos may not have convinced anybody, but the public

[1] *Guatemala: The Story of an Emergent Latin-American Democracy.*

laughed and applauded the general's spirit. When accused of being a
viejo enclenque, the sixty-four-year-old President went before the
cameras again and skipped rope. In short, he was *simpático*, a natural—
and on the stage he would have delighted millions, like Brendan Behan
or Jackie Gleason, for simply being himself.

The Problems of Miguel Ydígoras Fuentes

Unfortunately for Guatemala, Ydígoras was in politics. His political
career began promisingly enough when the old Ubiquista who had
been Ambassador to Great Britain returned to challenge Arbenz at the
polls. Whether Ydígoras would have won the 1950 election had it been
on the level—truckloads of government workers brandishing handfuls of
ballots had been shuttled from polling place to polling place—he was
forced to flee into exile as soon as the Arbenz victory was announced.
From El Salvador he plotted against the Communist regime, but when
Castillo Armas substituted authoritarianism of the Right for authoritarianism of the Left and refused to hold elections, Ydígoras retired
from the scene. Three years later, following Castillo Armas' assassination, he returned to run for the presidency a second time. He announced
that he expected to be counted out by fraud in the election of October
20, 1957—and apparently he was. The provisional government had run
its own candidate, and never in Guatemala's history had an unofficial
candidate won. But this time the irregularities had been too transparent.
A second election was held, and on March 15, 1958, Ydígoras Fuentes
began what should have been a six-year term as president.

From the beginning, Ydígoras was caught in a crossfire. The indus-
trial development that had taken place under Castillo Armas had been
at the expense of the social classes activated by the Arévalo-Arbenz
revolution—labor, the emergent middle class, the Indians. Millions in
American aid—this was before the Alliance for Progress' democratic
quid pro quo, of course—had helped. Ydígoras took some of the hand-
cuffs off the labor unions and tried to establish an income tax. This cost
him much of the support of the Right. But the austerity program that
he instituted in the wake of a disastrous fall in coffee prices that had
depleted the treasury's reserves, was followed by severe unemployment.
His name now became anathema to the Left.

This would probably have befallen Ydígoras anyway because of his
wholehearted backing of the United States' anti-Communist foreign
policy. There were provincial rebellions and threatened coups in the
capital, and Ydígoras responded to them in the time-honored way.
Guarantees of freedom of speech and press under the constitution were

revoked, and a state of siege was imposed. Castro was accused of arming guerrillas in the Puerto Barrios region, and soon it became known that Cuban exiles were being trained by the CIA at secret camps in Retalhuleu and the Petén. This offended Guatemalan nationalism, and Ydígoras was accused of being an American lackey. After the debacle at the Bay of Pigs, student strikes broke out, and two radical parties, one under Mario Méndez Montenegro and the other backing a return to power on the part of Juan Arévalo, began to gain adherents. Governmental corruption, on a scale unprecedented even for Guatemala, further undermined Ydígoras' personal popularity.

He Discovers the Belize Question

Frustrated at home and accused of making Guatemala a pawn of Big-Power politics abroad, Ydígoras attempted to revive his standing as a patriot by reopening the Belize Question—Guatemala's ancient claim to British Honduras.[2]

Historically, this is a claim not without substantial justice. Belize is the narrow Caribbean littoral running due south some three hundred miles from Mexico's Yucatán Peninsula almost to Puerto Barrios. It is bounded on the west by the jungle wastelands of the Petén and on the south by the Sarstoon River, which separates it from Guatemala's Izabál province. The Spaniards neglected this tropic lowland, since it was not readily accessible overland to either Mexico or Guatemala. But its long coastline exposed it to British naval power. Early in the seventeenth century British vessels from the islands off Honduras and Nicaragua where colonies already had been planted, came ashore, establishing trading posts to remove the valuable woods from the mountains of the interior. Slaves were imported in numbers far exceeding the whites, and escaped slaves from the Caribbean islands also took refuge in this no-man's-land. Their Negro descendants, with an admixture of Red Caribs from St. Vincent's Island, constitute the sparse population of the area to this day.

As the indigo trade developed, Spain and England became embroiled in endless diplomatic and naval maneuvers for the control of the territory, rich in logwood. After 1770, however, mahogany became the principal export, and since the Petén was virtually roadless, this precious wood was smuggled out of Guatemala on the Belize River, which cuts across Belize. A century and a half later, the market for mahogany yielded in turn to the market for sapodilla (chicle, the base of chewing

[2] Actually Ydígoras had first dabbled in this murky question while Ambassador to Great Britain during the early Arévalo period.

gum) and once more Belize became a haven for loggers and their con-
traband trade.

With the independence of Mexico and Central America from Spain,
the sovereignty of the territory had been open to two interpretations.
Mexico and Guatemala asserted their rights as inheritors of all lands
conquered by Spain. But since neither actually occupied the territory
at the time of independence, Britain declared that no claims deriving
from the act of revolution had any meaning. The British Navy, in any
event, was the only instrument of power operative in the area, so the
rival claims of Mexico and Guatemala were put forward only on paper.

In 1859 the government of Guatemala had decided to recognize
Great Britain's *de facto* colony by a treaty. Guatemala wanted British
naval help to contain the incursions of American filibusters like William
Walker. Belize was inaccessible to Guatemala. There was no conceiv-
able way of driving the settlers out. But as a matter of national pride
Guatemala insisted on a condition. The British must help build a road
connecting Guatemala City with the Caribbean.

It was agreed. In 1863 an additional convention to the treaty was
signed, defining the terms on which the road was to be built. But since
Guatemala was then at war, she did not come forward to ratify this
convention until a year later, and when she did Great Britain said:
Too late. It must be considered "most discreditable," says a British historian,[3] "for Britain thus to have taken advantage of the vagueness of
the wording of the treaty to evade payment of the 'inducement' to
which she had originally agreed when Guatemala renounced her pre-
tensions."

By the time Ydígoras Fuentes got around to reasserting Guatemala's
just historical claim, however, Belize was already well on the way to
becoming an independent nation—a nation that would tolerate continued economic and military ties with Great Britain only to thwart the
unwanted attentions of Guatemala and Mexico.

Belize Has Ideas of Its Own

How did this come about? No one who has visited Belize would go
so far as to call it a land with a promising economic future or a high
tourist potential. Its forest reserves have been virtually destroyed. Its
agricultural possibilities—in terms of growing fruits—are limited by its
very small size and relatively large population. Great Britain never did
much to build communications or industry—in fact Great Britain had

[3] *British Honduras: A Historical and Contemporary Survey*, by D. A. G.
Waddell. Oxford University Press, London, England, 1961.

for two centuries maintained its colony here reluctantly and continues to pay a large annual deficit only out of a sense of responsibility or commendable guilt. As tourist attractions there are the hundreds of off-shore *cayos*, a largely undeveloped paradise for fishermen and skin-divers, but not much else. Belize's Maya ruins cannot compare with those in the Petén or Yucatán. Native crafts are confined to the very small Indian enclave. There are no colonial buildings. The modern capital, a shantytown, is rebuilt every time there is a hurricane. "Hattie," in 1961, leveled Belize City.

Yet no one who has visited Belize has escaped its charm. Perhaps precisely because it has no romantic past to trade upon, it faces the future without regrets or illusions. Its people are friendly, humorous and spirited. They have *style*. The British traits of self-respect without blatant pride, honesty, cleanliness and fair play combine wonderfully well in Belize with such Negro traits as generosity, physical grace and uninhibited vivacity. Color prejudice does not exist. Class distinctions do tend to follow color lines, but lack of wealth is the only obstacle to the individual Negro's advancement.

Party politics and the movement for eventual independence began in Belize after World War II. The People's United Party (PUP) and its leader, George Price, who became First Minister in 1963, have dominated the little country ever since. In the early fifties, when part of the PUP favored the long-term British goal of associating Belize with the West Indies Federation, Price, because he opposed this prospect and favored association with Central America, was often accused of ties with Guatemala. Catholic, ascetic in private life, uncompromising and almost fanatical on the subject of giving his countrymen a sense of their Belizean identity, Price, as soon as Guatemala began to assert its claims aggressively, made his own position clear. He favors association with Central America on economic terms only; and since trade between Belize and Central America is negligible, even this is a remote ideal. Asked by the author recently to comment on Guatemala's and Mexico's claims, his answer was forthright:

> As far as I am aware, the Mexican government has decided not to press her alleged claims to this country unless the constitutional status quo is changed other than by independence. The Guatemalans have not withdrawn their alleged claim. We have made it clear to them that our goal is self-government within the Commonwealth and eventual independence, and that we want to evolve as an independent nation in our own right. Moreover we have made it clear that we shall ex-

pect all our neighbors to guarantee our sovereignty and respect our complete independence in keeping with the United Nations Charter.

Ydígoras Marches In and Out

The situation had come to a head in 1958, when Ydígoras Fuentes made his "symbolic" bid to enter Belize physically. He had come to the border at Benque Viejo with an armed retinue. Whether he expected the Belizeans to welcome him with open arms is not clear. A corporal on duty at the Customs House told the President he'd have to wait while he telephoned the Governor General for instructions. After a brief conversation, the corporal returned to the Guatemalan party and said: "I'm sorry. I have instructions to conduct you back across the frontier at once." He did just that, and the colonial administration in typical British fashion promoted him to sergeant for doing his duty.

Later on President Ydígoras revived the issue by claiming (untruthfully) that the United States Government had agreed to support Guatemala's claim to Belize in return for his help in providing camps for the Cuban exiles training for the Bay of Pigs invasion. But by that time Ydígoras had managed to offend most of his friends as well as his natural enemies.

The beginning of the end came on November 26, 1962, the day former President Arévalo announced his second candidacy. A revolt of right-wing air force officers was suppressed. But an anti-Arévalo committee threatened to try Arévalo for the Arana murder if he crossed the border. Ydígoras seemed to concur in this strategy when he announced in March that he had in his possession Arévalo's Communist Party card and that he was therefore ineligible to return. This decision, however, was overruled by the Supreme Court. Demonstrations and counterdemonstrations took place. Ydígoras made the mistake of accepting air reinforcements from the Nicaraguan dictator, Somoza. On March 31 Arévalo managed to cross the border and show up (briefly) in Guatemala City.

Colonel Peralta, the minister of defense, was quick to seize the opportunity. He took over the government; and from the Nicaraguan capital, whither the confused Ydígoras had fled, came the amazing statement that "What is going on in Guatemala is for its own good and for the good of the rest of Central America." Accused, understandably, of having connived or acquiesced in his own overthrow, Ydígoras later disowned the Peralta government, accusing his former defense minister of responsibility for Arévalo's sudden appearance and of having committed treason against Guatemalan democracy in the name of anti-Communism.[4]

Peralta's Coup and Military Dictatorship

The military government of Colonel Enrique Peralta Azurdia that ruled in Guatemala from the time of Ydígoras' overthrow until July of 1966, was heir to the same problems that beset Ydígoras and Castillo Armas. It faced them with as much honesty as the latter and more dignity than the former, but with as little attention to the root causes of Guatemala's distress as either.

Those who were surprised that the Peralta regime survived at all, and that Guatemala under his rule even registered modest economic progress, were perhaps laboring under two widespread misconceptions. One of these is that all Latin American states save Cuba are governed in behalf of a few wealthy families. The other is that the military establishments think only in terms of preserving the status quo. There is some truth in both propositions, but as absolutes they give rise to serious misconceptions. Unlike Panama or El Salvador, whose economies are dominated by a few wealthy families, or Nicaragua, which is the private preserve of one, Guatemala is not ruled by its millionaires. In fact, there are very few. The only family whose wealth in sugar and coffee lands dates back even as far as Barrios' time is the Herreras. Other wealthy families include the Castillos (brewing and hardware), the Hempsteads (coffee), the Pivaráls (cattle), the Weisenbergs (banking). Yet these families have never acted as a bloc—members of some of them even supported Arbenz; and Guatemala is probably the only Central American country save Costa Rica with a middle class whose wealth at least aggregates that of its oligarchs. Similarly with the military syndrome. In El Salvador the military, who are in power, have dictated social reforms that are opposed by most of the wealthy families. We have already seen how Colonel Arbenz and a considerable number of his fellow officers spearheaded the social revolution of the civilian professor Arévalo into its extreme phase. Colonel Castillo Armas, though he terminated that phase decisively, was frequently called a Communist by the extreme Right. Colonel Peralta, though never so accused, was a conservative rather than a reactionary; but time was running out on the conservative belief that industrialization and mere "stability" would themselves bring about social integration.

[4] *My War with Communism*, by Miguel Ydígoras Fuentes. Prentice-Hall, Inc., Englewood Cliffs, N.J., 1963.

Of the country's 4,500,000 inhabitants, 3,900,000 still live in the outback, most of them Indians and illiterate and all of them without a real stake in the capital's industries, banks and big plantations, which were experiencing a boom under Peralta. The income from coffee, cotton and bananas, almost doubling since Ydígoras' time, increased employment slightly, but not nearly enough to keep up with the birth rate and the drift of unemployables into the city. The emergent middle class (*ladinos*) continued to prey on the Indians but was not encouraged to join the cosmopolites. Lacking democratic institutions or even the independent trade unions of the Arévalo period, there was no way for this rootless class to put down roots or participate in important economic or political decisions. The student body at the University of San Carlos, for long Guatemala's only institution of higher learning, which might have been expected to provide leadership, was the victim of its own autonomy. Career students, with ten years of off-and-on attendance, were not uncommon. Radical politics and strikes were the norm, and attempts to achieve discipline by tightening entrance requirements and firing those who failed in examinations brought familiar charges of Yankee imperialism.

The spectacular failure of the government to eliminate a band of less than three hundred guerrilla rebels in the northeast corner of the country highlighted the extremely narrow base of popular support that Colonel Peralta enjoyed. Without widespread support in the countryside, such a minuscule band could not have survived.

Guerrilla Country: Lake Izabál

Lake Izabál is a large and shallow pear-shaped body of water connected to the Caribbean by a deeply gorged outlet, the Rio Dulce. As far back as the sixteenth century its strategic value was recognized. Enemy intruders, entering the lake and then the Polochíc River at its western extremity, which is navigable part of the way to Cobán, could have penetrated dangerously close to the capital. A fort was therefore built in the jungle where the Rio Dulce is narrowest, and a chain was stretched across to keep pirates out.

Today the scenic gorge, the restored fortress of San Felipe and the lake with its tarpon and whale-size manatees are tourist attractions—or would be, if the more purposeful pirates of our time hadn't found the region perfectly suited to their sanctuary. The avenues of intrusion, of course, have shifted from the visible waterways to the impenetrable jungles on both sides of the lake, and the forbidding mountains behind. And the strategic goals are now Puerto Matias de Galvez and Puerto

Barrios, Guatemala's Caribbean ports, and the Atlantic Highway, which Arbenz began and Castillo Armas finished, linking the port and the capital. The "enemy" was no longer Sir Francis Drake or Henry Morgan, but Lieutenant Marco Antonio Yon Sosa, late of the Guatemalan Army, graduate of the United States' Counterinsurgency School at Panama, and his elusive Communist-oriented guerrillas.

Yon Sosa's career as a revolutionary of the Left began under Ydígoras in 1960 when he quit the army to take part in an abortive rebellion. On February 13, 1962, the voice of Jacobo Arbenz was heard over Radio Havana announcing: "A week ago today a handful of young patriots embarked on the glorious path of guerrilla warfare. Their movement . . . will end the rotted regime of the criminal traitors, accomplices of the corrupt and tyrannical Miguel Ydígoras Fuentes." Yon Sosa and his latter-day highwaymen had already captured a military outpost at Mariscos on the lake, and advancing eastward across the highway and the Motagua River they had hijacked eighteen thousand dollars from the company safe at Bananera, capital of United Fruit's ailing empire.

The action had propaganda value far in excess of its monetary one. Yon Sosa was giving notice to his countrymen that the Arévalo-Arbenz revolution had not died and that American imperialist interests would continue to be the primary targets. Bananera, where the white foreigners with their segregated luxury facilities lived in a world apart from the native workers in their crowded barracks,[5] was the perfect symbolic target. It did not matter that United Fruit had long since turned over to the government of Guatemala thousands of acres at Tiquisate to be distributed among the landless. It did not matter that Bananera itself had fallen into decay and that the company had shifted most of its business to Ecuador, where it buys bananas directly from native producers. It did not matter that the Alliance for Progress had superseded Dollar Diplomacy.

The Challenge of Communism

In 1966 Yon Sosa, despite repeated campaigns by the Peralta military to run him down, was still at large—a Robin Hood to the dispossessed who supplied and concealed him in the outback, a terrorist to the ruling caste in the capital who felt the financial squeeze of his kidnappings for ransom and the thud of his demolition charges by night. In 1965 an NBC camera team had run Yon Sosa down. In the Sierra de

[5] See Chapter 4, p. 54.

las Minas back of Lake Izabál he was asked why he opposed United States policy under the Alliance for Progress. His answer was:

> I believe the Alliance for Progress was inspired by good intentions, but it is too late. In order to function at all, the Alliance needs certain basic preconditions—the tax reform, agrarian reform. But as soon as these reforms are attempted the ruling classes, the oligarchy, the large landowners begin to maneuver against them. They stop all progress. How can we make progress peacefully? It is impossible.

A government whose goals are negative perforce expends its resources and energies on peripheral problems. It concentrates on holding Communists at arm's length—as though this were nothing more than a military problem. It endeavors to guarantee the prerogatives of the absentee landlords, regardless of whether the economy progresses or languishes by such a policy. It even goes out of its way to block loans and technical assistance from its friends, lest it be accused later of dependency or treason.

It may seek to replace politicians in the civil service with trained personnel. It may try to eliminate the standard *mordida* in government contracts. It may move against notorious corruption in the administration of the *fincas nacionales*. To stimulate local self-government, it may give a soupçon of authority to the regional governments and a degree of autonomy to the *municipios*. (Though in this it is hamstrung by its own failure to loosen the national grip on the budget; for what does autonomy mean without funds for community development?) It may improve communications, sanitation, health.[6] It may build schools (inadequately staffed, almost always) and thus lower by a few percentage points the nation's 70 percent illiteracy. It may recognize the language barrier to integration by insisting on two years of Spanish in the Indian curriculum.

But what good is Spanish to an Indian under present conditions? Will it give him land? Will it give him cheap, long-term credits for the purchase of seed, fertilizers and equipment? Will it give him storage, market and irrigation facilities, or the farm-to-market roads on which he can move his produce before it rots? Will it give him the franchise? And what good is the government's awareness that the economy's fatal susceptibility to fluctuations in the international price of coffee can

[6] Life expectancy in Guatemala is forty-three years, as compared to sixty-eight in the United States. But everyone knows by now, with India's example in plain view, that improving health without lowering the birth rate means taking two steps backward for every one forward.

only be remedied by diversified and self-sustaining crops, if those who control the country's most fertile lands stand to make quicker profits in cotton?

The interests represented by the military dictatorship of the oligarchy were a tiny minority. Those involved in Yon Sosa's band were an even tinier minority. By 1965 a rival movement led by Luis Túrcios, a twenty-four-year-old commander, and Bernardo Alvarado Monzón was calling itself the Rebel Armed Forces. In 1966 this guerrilla band seemed to have taken the play away from its rival, granting interviews and pictures to enterprising American newsmen, carrying out spectacular kidnappings of wealthy Guatemalans for ransom, and so on. On July 1, 1966, these leaders issued a statement charging the Peralta regime with twenty-eight political "murders" and, although not declaring war on the new government of Julio César Mendez Montenegro, stating that the Army "is still the same reactionary tool of native plutocracy and foreign companies and therefore must be fought to the bitter end." [7] But for the oligarchy time was running out. Either the *ladinos* will have their way, as they were beginning to in 1950–54, or the Indians will have theirs. This is Guatemala's special problem and a unique one: the confrontation of two ways of life that has been building up for five centuries. Is any accommodation between the two possible?

Guatemala's Dilemma: Ladinos *and/or* Indians?

The easier way out—and the necessary if not inevitable one, most sociologists think—is to speed up the slow process of *ladino*-ization. Move in, these thinkers say, on the isolated, scattered Indian families and their backward settlements. Shame them into discarding their colorful but divisive costumes for Western clothes. Encourage the Church (or the State) to root out paganism. Substitute Spanish for the babel of pre-Columbian tongues. Above all, propagandize the Indian into *wanting things* he presently has no use for—beginning with shoes and chemical fertilizers and proceeding eventually to refrigerators, toilets, television sets and cars. Once the Indian is forced to think that he needs these things and is entitled to them, the argument goes, progress will follow.

[7] On October 2, 1966, Túrcios was killed in an automobile accident on the road between Antigua and the capital. Leadership of the Rebel Armed Forces was assumed by César Montes. Túrcios, like Yon Sosa, had received his commando training in the United States. His movement was backed by Moscow and Havana; Yon Sosa's group by Peking.

There is a certain arrogance inherent in this argument. The assumption that the Indian will be better off and "happier" with what *we* want him to have is related to another assumption—that democracy, American democracy, will automatically result if one teaches a man how to read and write. Even some of its most convinced proponents are uneasy about the consequences of *ladino*-ization, like the man who said: "Of course we have to change them, but for God's sake let's not talk or think about what we're changing them into!"

The minority view, which is concerned about mechanically substituting an ugly, efficient, unhappy way of life for a beautiful, inefficient, tolerable one, begins by weighing the pros and cons of Indian and *ladino* traits—here and now. Folkways and handicrafts aside, the Indian has values and a morality of his own. He is basically honest. His ties to family and community are deep. The philosophy of the *cofradía* is profoundly democratic: no one is told what to do or denounced for not doing it or doing it badly; each man feels the responsibility *within himself*. It would be difficult for an Indian to become a dictator unless he were *ladino*-ized. He doesn't think in terms of exploiting others.

The *ladino*, on the other hand, is a loner. He has no community feeling at all—witness the filth and brutishness of a city like Escuintla. His loyalty is first to himself, then (a little) to his family, then—nothing. His basic premise, that there is no one a man can trust, makes for very slow progress. His gnawing fear, once he has "passed over" from the Indian world, is that he may be drawn back or inadvertently reveal his humble origin. Nor does he have any pride of caste, in being a *ladino*, except vis-à-vis the Indian. The lowliest clerk or stenographer would be deeply insulted if called *ladino*, identifying rather with the boss or the socialite. The *ladino*'s spiritual capitals are places he has never seen and never will see: Madrid or Hollywood.

There are intellectuals in Guatemala who would not like to see Guatemala homogenized. This minority thinks that Indian culture is the original and most valuable ingredient in the nation's society. It believes that the way out lies through education. The Indian is vulnerable to *ladino*-ization only because he has an ingrained reverence for authority (Church or State), because he drinks (taking no pleasure in it) to escape the fatality of his situation, and because he takes little conscious pride in his culture. Those who believe he can be educated to take such a pride point out that integration has never been an Indian goal, and that although it is claimed to be the *ladino* goal, it is in fact a threat to the *ladino*'s very existence, to his ego; for if integration were achieved, whom would he exploit?

The correct approach, these educators say, is to achieve a *Guate-*

malan culture, with Indians and *ladinos* each allowed, by government decree, to develop in his own way. Recent governments have not brought about a unified culture. Their declared policy of "assimilation" has failed. Official American aid organizations have not been in touch with the Indians. Only the Peace Corps has lived in the Indian community—and believes in it; though directives from Washington are constantly exhorting corpsmen to remember that the *ladino* rides the wave of the future. Church and private organizations work with the Indians but not on a scale to make much impact.

Indianists, Guatemalan or American, agree that the Indian must be brought into the larger economy; but they insist that he must be brought in *as an Indian*, not as a potential *ladino*. This means teaching him to read and write in his own languages and making Spanish available only if he wants it. Life for the Indian in a *ladino* school has been a nightmare; he is ridiculed, made to feel inferior. Conversely, *ladinos* must have their own schools, for they in turn are frustrated and held back when educated with Indians.

Only when such a policy is adopted officially, these nonconformists feel, will there be an end to the disastrous antagonism made manifest in the *ladino* saying: "Every Indian a *mozo*, every *ladino* a *patrón*." Only then will it be possible for the social revolution to move forward democratically, without interference from Russians, Cubans, or Americans, as an indigenous Guatemalan movement toward a better life. Only then will tradition be fertilized by the present to achieve continuity. Only then will the merely picturesque be ennobled and the humble craftsman become a proud creator. Only then will the land and the people be one.

After Peralta

In the general election of March 6, 1966, the Revolutionary Party headed by Julio César Mendez Montenegro and Clemente Marroquín Rojas won 209,204 votes out of a total of 531,281 ballots cast, thus defeating the Peralta-backed slate of Colonel Juan de Dios Aguilár de León and Gustavo Miron Porras, whose Institutional Democratic Party ran second with 148,015. In the resulting runoff election held in the Congress May 10, the Revolutionary Party presidential candidates won by 35 to 19. Mendez Montenegro, one of whose brothers was killed by Castillo Armas' Liberation Army, won despite charges that he was anti-American on that account and that the Law School, of which he had been dean, harbored Communist intellectuals. Marroquín Rojas has had a long career in Guatemalan politics. Exiled by Ubico, he returned to serve as Minister of Economy under Arévalo. He supported Castillo Armas and then denounced him. The editorials in his lively newspaper *La Hora* have taken extremist positions on all the political, economic and racial questions of the twentieth century.

The Revolutionary Party is said to represent the moderate center, but under these mercurial leaders Guatemala's future direction is hard to predict.

Part II
ILLUSTRATIONS

Photo: Joya Hairs

PLATE 1. Early Classic Maya stela, Kaminal Juyú (National Archaeological Museum, Guatemala City).

PLATE 2. Copy by Antonio Tejeda Fonseca of lost Classic Maya fresco, Uaxactún (National Archaeological Museum).

Photo: George Holton

Photo: Author

PLATE 3. Temple I, Tikál, with stelae. Restoration by University of Pennsylvania archaeologists.

Photo: Irving Whitman

PLATE 4. Zoomorph "P," Quiriguá.

PLATE 5. Dale Nichols taking a rubbing from Maya relief at El Baúl.

Courtesy: Dale Nichols

PLATE 6. Detail Stela 11, Seibal; late Classic period.

Photo: George Holton

PLATE 7. Daniel Schafer in ruin of Quiché Maya capital, Utatlán, destroyed by Alvarado.

PLATE 8. Façade of cathedral in Ciudad Vieja (near Antigua), early colonial capital.

Photo: Author

PLATE 9. Ruin of domeless crossing in the earthquake-shattered cathedral, Antigua.

PLATE 10. Market with sunshades, San Francisco el Alto.

Photo: Author

Photo: Julio Zadik

PLATE 11. Guatemala City, showing cathedral, national palace, and, in distance, Fuego volcano.

PLATE 12. Relief panels on Crédito Hipotecario, Guatemala City, by Efraín Recinos (1964).

Photo: Sittler

Photo: Author

PLATES 13 AND 14. Street advertisements, Guatemala City (1965).

Photo: Author

PLATE 15. Burning copal on the church steps, Chichicastenango.

PLATE 16. Invocation and sacrifice to the Maya idol outside Chichicastenango.

PLATE 17. Dance of the Conquest, Sololá Fiesta, August 15.

PLATE 18. Street sign for a hardware shop, Chichicastenango.

PLATE 19. Displaying an embroidered male head-shawl (*zut*) in the square at Nahualá.

PLATE 20. Woolen Indian jackets with appliquéd bat design, Sololá.

Photo: Author

PLATE 21. Mother and child with embroidered *huipils*, Nahualá.

PLATE 22. Indian flute and drum combine on the church steps, San Raimundo.

Photo: Author

Photo: Author

PLATE 23. View of the basilica, Esquipulas.

PLATE 24. View of Cobán from Calvario church steps. Note pagan shrine in pillar.

Photo: Author

Photo: George Holton

PLATE 25. Saturday night bath in the hot springs, Momoste-nango.

PLATE 26. Dugout canoes on the Subín River near Sayaxché, Petén.

Photo: Joya Hairs

PLATE 27. President General Don Jorge Ubico, *c*. 1940.

Courtesy: Raúl Gonzáles, El Imparciál.

Courtesy: Raúl Gonzáles, El Imparciál.

PLATE 28. President Juan José Arévalo, *c*. 1947.

Courtesy: Raúl Gonzáles, El Imparciál.

PLATE 29. President Jacobo Arbenz (left) at a diplomatic reception, *c.* 1952.

Courtesy: Raúl Gonzáles, El Imparciál.

PLATE 30. President Miguel Ydígoras Fuentes casting his ballot, *c.* 1960.

PLATE 31. Policeman near Government House, Belize City, Belize, 1965.

Photo: Author

PLATE 32. Premier George Price (left) with former Under Secretary of Colonies Nigel Fisher at self-government celebrations, Punta Gorda, Belize. Note Kekchi Indians in long skirts (right).

Courtesy: Raúl Gonzáles, El Imparciál.

Part III
TRAVELOGUE

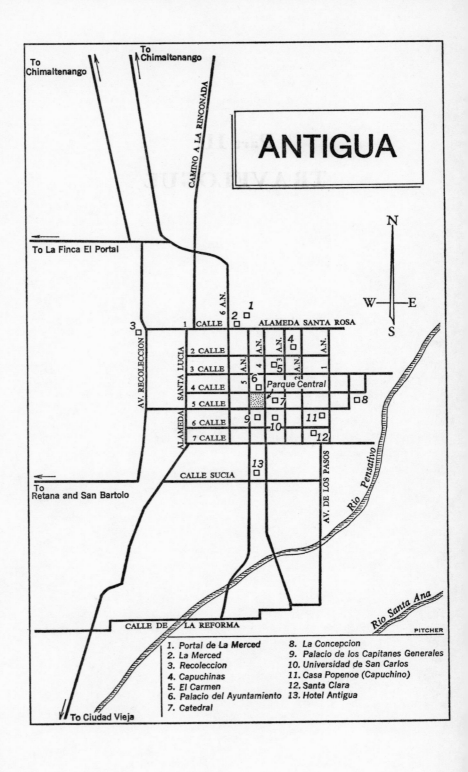

ANTIGUA

N
W — E
S

To Chimaltenango
To Chimaltenango
To Chimaltenango

CAMINO A LA RINCONADA

To La Finca El Portal

6 A.N.

1
2 □
1 CALLE   ALAMEDA SANTA ROSA

3 □   2 CALLE   *4*
AV. RECOLECCION   SANTA LUCIA   3 CALLE   *5*   1
A.N.   4   3 A.N.
A.N.   4 A.N.

4 CALLE   *6* □   Parque Central
5   *7* □

ALAMEDA   5 CALLE   □ *8*

6 CALLE   *9* □   *11* □
10   □

7 CALLE   □ *12*

To
Retana and San Bartolo

13
CALLE SUCIA   □

AV. DE LOS PASOS

Rio Pensativo

Rio Santa Ana

PITCHER

CALLE DE LA REFORMA

To Ciudad Vieja

1. Portal de La Merced
2. La Merced
3. Recoleccion
4. Capuchinas
5. El Carmen
6. Palacio del Ayuntamiento
7. Catedral
8. La Concepcion
9. Palacio de los Capitanes Generales
10. Universidad de San Carlos
11. Casa Popenoe (Capuchino)
12. Santa Clara
13. Hotel Antigua

Tourists

DURING the winter of 1965 the magazine *Newsweek* published a report entitled "Guatemala: The Non-Tourist Industry." Conceding that "mile for mile, Guatemala probably contains more natural tourist attractions than any other country in the Western Hemisphere," the article observed that Guatemala was earning only $2.6 million a year from American tourists (compared to $34 million for nearby Panama, for example). The reasons for this were alleged to be humiliating vigilance on the part of customs inspectors looking for Communist spies; red tape that was blocking issuance of a single tourist card good for all the Central American countries; "indifferent" food; "second class" hotels; and "impassable" roads. "The odds are," *Newsweek* concluded, "that it will be a long time before gringo tourists get that reassuring feeling of being wanted in Guatemala."

Having spent the same winter traveling in every part of Guatemala and having entered and left the country six times in that period, the author would like to modify this fairly common view. Let it be said first that *one* of the reasons Guatemala continues to contain more tourist attractions than any other Western Hemisphere country is precisely that its hotels and food are modest and its *secondary* roads (rarely impassable) are unpaved. Guatemala, in other words, is not for those who go abroad to do what can be done just as well at home. It does not have gambling casinos and opulent nightclubs, and though it does have bathing beaches, swimming pools, tennis and golf, no one would pretend that in these appurtenances of the American Way of Life it can rival Palm Springs or Miami Beach, San Juan or Montego Bay, Nassau or Bermuda. These expensive resorts, on the other hand, are notably sterile in the arts of past and present, and they have nothing at all to offer in the way of exploration or adventure.

There is no question that a multicountry tourist card for Central America would be a boon, but if Americans are subjected to harassment in matters of political allegiance this traveler did not encounter it. (There is, to be sure, a curious customs declaration that reads: "You may bring in duty free the following: Books, Manuscripts, 100 Grams of Elaborated Tobacco, Photographic Pictures Non-Commercial, Food for Infants and Sick Persons for Consumption on the Trip, Night Underwear, Table Cloths Already Used, One Sewing Machine *or* One Typewriter, and One Calculator Machine When the Passenger is Over 18 Years Old.")

Compared at least to Mexico, where *gringos* are generally mistrusted and sometimes heckled, Guatemala's friendliness to Americans is immediately noticeable. This is as true among the remote Indian villages of the highlands as it is in the capital. Asked why, an American of many years' residence replied with a smile: "Perhaps because to Guatemalans the Colossus of the North has been traditionally—Mexico."

Hotels and Cars

Because of the country's relatively small size, the number of good hotels in Guatemala is not a problem. The capital has a dozen moderately priced, clean and with good food, and one luxury establishment, the Guatemala Biltmore, which has everything. At the western extremity of the highlands, a day's drive from the capital, is Quezaltenango, and there the Pensión Bonifáz is first-rate and serves the best food in Central America. A little to the north of this city is Huehuetenango, surrounded by almost as many accessible attractions, and this city is well served by the Hotel Zaculeu. Cobán's two inns, La Posada and the Monja Blanca, are more modest but comfortable. If one continues on (all routes will soon be described) to Livingston on the Caribbean, the Del Mar is the place to stay; and at Puerto Barrios the Del Norte. At Chichicastenango, the Mayan Inn is expensive but superbly furnished with its owner's collection of antiques; it is memorable, too, for its service in local costume and for its cuisine. The Number One hotel at Panajachel on Lake Atitlán is the Tzanjuyú, but there are half a dozen smaller ones that are quite good, of which the Monterrey is notable both for its lakeside location and its reasonable rates. There is one first-class hotel with a swimming pool at Antigua, the Antigua, and again a half-dozen first-rate pensions. Tikál, in the heart of the Petén and accessible only by air, has a Jungle Lodge with family-size bungalows. The Pacific beach resort of San José, though it has no hotels that can be recommended, does have the several dozen well-equipped cabañas of Don Mañuel Uruela at Chulamár, which may be rented by the day or for longer.

For visitors who come to Guatemala without their car, there are two ways to see the countryside. One is by bus. Buses run on schedule. To Antigua, for example, they go every hour and the fare is only ninety cents. The other way is via the capital's various auto-rental agencies. To rent a Hertz Volkswagen for a weekend circuit (Saturday morning through Monday) of Lake Atitlán and Antigua costs about fifty dollars. For a whole week—including a 400-kilometer trip to Atitlán and Chichicastenango, as well as to Antigua—the price is in the neighborhood of $100. Only an American driver's license is required.

Guatemala City

Since all of Guatemala's principal cities and major attractions (outside of the Petén) are within a one-day's drive or less of the capital, we will assume that the visitor makes Guatemala City his base. The capital is neither ancient and beautiful, in the sense of Antigua, nor picturesque and exotic, as Quezaltenango or Chichicastenango; but it is spacious and cosmopolitan, and at its 4897-foot elevation in a narrow valley surrounded by mountains, wonderfully healthful.

The streets are laid out at right angles and numbered. The *Avenidas* run north and south. The *Calles*—at least in Zone 1—run east and west. Zone 1 is the northernmost and oldest part of the city; here are the shopping center, most of the hotels and theaters and churches, the presidential palace and the American Embassy. Sixth Avenida, with its kaleidoscopic jungle of shops and neon signs, is the east-west dividing line; it runs through the Parque Central and then connects with the Avenida Bolívar running southwest to the Trebol. If followed straight through this junction point, Bolívar becomes the road to Lake Amatitlán, Escuintla, San José and the Pacific. But the road *crossing* Bolívar at the Trebol is the Inter-American Highway, running west to Lake Atitlán, Chichicastenango, Quezaltenango and the Mexican border, east to El Salvador. Turning *right* on it (at the Trebol), one passes the Roosevelt Hospital, the ruins of Kaminal Juyú (see Chapter 1, p. 4), the branch road to Antigua, and so on, into the highlands. Turning *left*, one passes the Zoological Park, the Museums of Natural History and Archaeology, the National Hippodrome, and the Airport.

A more direct route from the Old City to the Airport, however, is provided by 10th Avenida, which becomes spacious, tree-shaded Avenida Reforma, bisecting the city's residential district (Zones 9 and 10) and passing the Hotel Guatemala Biltmore before turning into Avenida Las Americas, paralleling the Airport.

Just south of the Old City and flanked by these two major arteries (Bolívar and Reforma) before they diverge on their ways to the Trebol and the Airport, is a complex of splendid modern buildings. The complex is tucked in between an ancient fort with new outdoor and indoor theaters on a hill to the west and the Olympic Stadium with its public swimming pool and tennis courts to the east. In or on these new buildings is to be seen the finest that Guatemala has to offer in the way of modern art: colorful semiabstract mosaics by Guatemala's most famous painter, Carlos Mérida; monumental relief sculpture, many stories high, by Efraín Recinos and Roberto Gonzalez Goyri. The amphitheater, high on the fortified hill, is appropriately embellished with poured-concrete bastions designed by the multitalented Recinos. (See Plate 12.)

Returning to the Old City, the cathedral and the churches of San Francisco and La Mercéd are worth a visit. So is the Mercado Central, the enormous enclosed market behind the cathedral where almost everything grown and made by the Indians is to be found. Collectors have gone to Chinautla, a tiny village of potters six miles north of the city, in search of ceramic figurines, only to discover that the booth of Doña María in the Mercado is the one place where these angels with bell-like skirts and groups of peasant worshipers may be purchased. This is the place to note in passing, too, that the finest of Guatemala's incomparable Indian textiles are not to be found in the capital's gift shops; they may be acquired—from proud possessors who are never eager, and often unwilling, to sell them—only in the villages (Nahualá, San Raimundo, Totonicapán, Santiago Atitlán, San Francisco El Alto, Chichicastenango, Zuñíl, etc.) where they are woven for everyday use. This applies also to the famous bat-wing jackets (see Plate 20) and knitted bags of Sololá, but it does not apply to Momostenango's great woolen blankets, which are marketed by street vendors all over Guatemala at prices hardly in excess of those charged in Momostenango itself. The only popular art indigenous to the capital, and rarely rivaled in the provinces, is the painting of signs. (See Plates 13, 14, 18.)

North of the Old City, in the Parque Minerva, is the monumental relief map of Guatemala covering more than 2500 square meters and constructed by the engineer Francisco Vela in 1905. Every volcano, river and lake is identified by a small tin flag, but unless one comes here with a pretty fair knowledge of Guatemala's deeply wrinkled terrain, this is a place to become confused rather than oriented.

Equally confusing is the way out of Guatemala City to the Atlantic

Highway, Cobán and Puerto Barrios. The highway emerges out of this maze of streets surrounding the Parque Minerva. It can be found by resort to constant inquiry, but it cannot be described. Eventually one comes to a bridge over a yawning *barranco*—a favorite spot for the suicides of discarded soccer heroes, so they say—and from there on there are no problems.

The two museums already mentioned must not be missed.

The Museum of Natural History is a monument to the enterprise, efficiency and good taste of one man, its founder and director, Jorge Ibarra. Without any funds for acquisition, Señor Ibarra has put together a superb display of mounted birds and beasts, every item clearly dated and identified, in glass display cases with painted backdrops. General Ubico bequeathed a ten-foot crocodile he shot in the Rio Dulce. Castillo Armas contributed an ocelot. The complete elephant's skeleton (one of the few nonindigenous exhibits) was wired together by the director from a sack of bones someone mailed him from India.

The Museum of Archaeology contains probably the finest collection of Maya sculpture in the world, but its presentation (uncatalogued, undated, and largely unidentified) is so chaotic that no one but an archaeologist could find his way around or be sure of what he was looking at. Its director since 1948 has been Antonio Tejeda Fonseca. The budget (apart from the salaries of a staff of ten, including guards) is forty dollars a month; the director estimates that a minimum of twenty thousand dollars would be needed to catalogue and adequately display the collection. Señor Tejeda painted the scale watercolor of the lost Uaxactún fresco mentioned in Chapter 1, and also the handsome copy of one of the Bonampák frescoes in the lobby of the Guatemala Biltmore Hotel. Possibly the museum's finest piece is a painted bowl found intact at Altar de Sacrificios in the Petén; but the stelae from Piedras Negras and Kaminal Juyú are also major works of art, and the relief from the former site is unique in its realism. The Piedras Negras masterpieces were brought here, Guatemalans say, to prevent the Mexicans across the river from stealing them. British and German museum hawks had already made off with the finest carved wood lintels from Tikál.

Antigua

A pleasant hour's drive southwest of the city lies the restored colonial capital, Antigua, whose evolution and destruction was described in Chapter 2. It is overrun by guides, and vendors of an incredible variety of fakes but is not to be avoided for all that. Its Hotel Antigua is elegant, its gift shops (Pat Crocker, Eva Hannstein de Smith, others) are the best in Guatemala, its restorations are almost as pleasant to look at as its ruins. Ciudad Vieja, the earlier capital, four miles to the southeast, is a more subdued antique. (See Plate 8.)

The splendid shell of Antigua's cathedral has already been mentioned (P. 28, Plate 9).

The Palace of the Captains-General is a long, handsome arcaded building, often rebuilt and restored; it now contains the Governor's office and other municipal agencies. The University of San Carlos Borromeo, just off the Plaza, is a Spanish-Moorish building with an impressive patio and a museum of paintings and relics from the colonial period.

The Church of Our Lady of La Mercéd—from which the great Easter parade headed by the figure of Christ carrying His Cross still emerges on its slow regal progress to the Mayor's Palace—survived the various earthquakes of the eighteenth century almost intact. Its yellow façade, appliquéd in white stucco with vines, flowers and abstract motifs, is a masterpiece of the churrigueresque. Its sculptured fountain, where the Brothers once carried out experiments in fish breeding, is the finest in Guatemala.

Dwarfing even the cathedral in size were the two great churches of Santo Domingo and San Francisco at either end of the Calle de la Nobleza. Las Casas was the first vicar of Santo Domingo, but what he would have thought of the opulence for which its church and convent soon became famous may be imagined. Thomas Gage in the next century described a life-size Virgin in solid silver, a silver lamp before the altar so heavy that it required three monks to raise and lower it and a paved fishing pond a quarter of a mile long for the friars' recreation and cuisine. The Franciscan church was hardly less Lucullan. Its single high nave and massive golden domes were a challenge to earthquakes that Nature was quick to accept. But the architectural grandeur now mellowed by ruin once framed such tasteless *objets d'art* as an Ecce Homo in cork with glass eyes (now in the capital); and it may once have been such flagrant disregard for the teachings of the humble Fisherman of Galilee that drove the famous Franciscan, Pedro de Betancourt, to envision an order (Bethlehemites) pledged to carry the sick on their backs, and his noble successor, Don Rodrigo de Arias Maldonado, to give up careers in Indian "pacification" and love-making.

Other notable churches, still to be seen in something of their original splendor, are those of La Recolección and of our Lady of Carmen. But more interesting still are the fabulous convents and monasteries, Las Capuchinas, Santa Clara, and La Concepción. Visitors to the first never fail to marvel at the two stories of cells for novices and nuns, radiating from a circular chamber in the cloister, each cell with its own bathroom and sewage conduits. Santa Clara's massive patio fountain, enclosed by a double tier of arches, is today a favorite spot for picnickers and photographers. First and richest of all the colonial capital's convents, La Concepción has already been mentioned. (See Pp. 28–29.)

Most celebrated of the restored colonial homes in Antigua is the Casa del Capuchino, owned by Wilson Popenoe. It was restored and furnished during the early 1930's by the American agronomist's first wife, the late Dorothy Popenoe, and became the subject of a charming book, Louis Adamic's *The House in Antigua*. The Popenoe house is much more than a demonstration, in perfect taste, of how the master class lived in the 1650's. It is—and this seems to be the point of Adamic's book—an example of how perfection can be re-created out of wreckage, the past brought back to life, the future illuminated. Dorothy Popenoe was an archaeologist. She had a will to create something beautiful and permanent, a will that had hardly existed in Guatemala since the destruction of Antigua; and not being an artist, she determined to invoke the creativeness of the past. Her restoration was an act of love, in which her husband, a creative scientist, fully participated. But Wilson Popenoe came to realize that it is the Indians—not the descendants of the Conquistadors whose arrogance, austere pride and fanatical religiosity are mirrored in Antigua—who hold the keys to a rebirth of the creative spirit in Guatemala.[1]

Antigua has many fiestas, but those taking place during Lent and Holy Week are outstanding. At 8 A.M. on Good Friday the images of the Virgin and the Saints begin to emerge from the massive, ornate portal of La Mercéd to the roll of drums. Musicians with trumpets in gaudy red and yellow costumes are stationed high atop the yellow façade. The gigantic figure of Christ, bent under a crucifix newly fashioned of pine trunks, is mounted on a catafalque perhaps twenty-four feet long and four feet wide covered with waves of gray metal to simulate earth, out of which artificial flowers and cactus "grow." Sixty men are required to carry this one image, each having his own leather padding and number plate on the rails. Since they work in ten shifts, a total of six hundred uniformed honorary pallbearers are employed; 2200 other marchers in costume—bearers, centurions, musicians, incense-swingers—make up the parade. Other floats support life-size images of Christ with a Flayed Back, Christ Chained to a Blood-

[1] The author's discussion of this question with Dr. Popenoe is contained in Chapter 4 of *The Road to Panama*, Hawthorn Books, Inc., New York, 1966.

Spattered Column, the Virgin Waving Veronica's Veil, etc. Judas hangs from the branch of a high tree along the way.

The procession, as it winds its way about the city, passes over a series of multicolored sawdust "rugs," their intricate floral-symbolic patterns laid down on the cobblestones in advance by experts who sift the various colors through cardboard cutouts like cookie molds. At 2 P.M., when Christ's image passes over the "rug" in front of the Municipal Building, it is traditional for lots to be drawn on the balcony and a single prisoner from the city's jail to be released unconditionally. In 1965 the prisoners were there, singing devotional chants as always; but when one of them was presented with the wreath and came forward to lay it at the feet of Christ the Pardoner, he was promptly escorted back to jail by the police. There were those who said that Colonel Peralta's frantic search for subversives had triumphed over Christ's mercy.

Paradox has always triumphed at Antigua, paradox with a hint of things to come. Long before the basilica with its five naves, sixteen chapels and sixty-eight vaults caved in, burying the tombs of Alvarado and his proud mate in rubble, the city's prophetic symbol-makers had chosen an appropriate coat-of-arms: St. James on a charger poised over the three volcanoes, the one in the center already capped with its warning mushroom cloud.

The Road to Quezaltenango

Continuing past the Antigua cutoff, the Inter-American Highway winds its way westward two hundred kilometers along the top of the highlands to Quezaltenango, Guatemala's second city. To visit on a day's trip, or even to describe, all the Indian villages branching off this highway would be impossible. If the trip is to be made in a day, the motorist is advised to stop for lunch at the Swiss-chalet-like Restaurant Katók (Cakchiquel for "Welcome") at Kilometer Marker 87 near Tecpán. Paulino Jarquín, Nicaragua-born and Oregon-educated, is the proprietor, and he stocks the excellent larder from his own nearby farm. If he can be induced to leave, he is also the best of guides to the Thursday market at Tecpán and the ruins of Iximché (see Chapter 2, pp. 22–23) just off the road. Jarquín's marimba combine, the Arco-Iris-Infantíl, supplies the best native music in Guatemala.

On the morning leg of the trip (with a very early start) there might be time to visit one of the following Indian villages: San Juan Sacatepequez, San Lucas Sacatepequez, Santiago Sacatepequez, or Comalapa. Since the first is close to Guatemala City and a good hour's drive off the highway, it had better be visited from the capital itself. Another advantage in so doing is that other villages farther up this branch road (Route 5, north to Rabinál) are still more interesting. The Sunday market and the costumes at San Raimundo are delightful; and then there are the ruins of the Pocomán capital at Mixco Viejo, and far to the north Rabinál with its oranges and rice paddies in a cuplike valley. The Restaurant Villa Olga, 29 kilometers north of the capital on this road, does a rushing business Sundays; it is run by an ex-GI, Sergeant Samuel Milligan, who married a Guatemalan in New Orleans and brought his collection of Chinese curios from Taiwan with him when he settled here.

The twin villages of Santiago Sacatepequez and San Lucas Sacatepequez lie just off the highway not far from the capital. Peace between them is shaky. The church of the latter is almost always locked. It contains the image of a white dog with black spots, somewhat resembling the one in the old Victor phonograph ads. During a plague many years ago the villagers heard of the miraculous powers of a certain dog-image in Spain and ordered an exact replica. It worked. But some fifty years later Santiago Sacatepequez was visited by a plague of its own, and after much negotiation managed to borrow San Lucas' dog. Again there were miraculous cures, but Santiago refused to return the image. When negotiations failed, the angry citizens of San Lucas stormed the church at Santiago, returned the dog to their own church —and padlocked the doors.

Comalapa, an hour's drive north of the highway on a dirt road west of Chimaltenango, boasts one of the richest and loveliest churches in Guatemala—and two of the country's three "primitive" painters. The Church of San Juan Bautista, dating from 1600, is notable for a collection of lamps and silver ornaments that the *cofrades* have been wise to guard jealously. They are a resplendent sight during the fiestas (St. John, June 24; the Immaculate Conception, December 8; and the Virgin of Guadalupe, December 12). The sculptures in the niches of this church's noble façade are repainted in brilliant colors every few years. The two primitive painters, Andrés Curuchich and Santiago Tuctuc, sell their pictures at their homes nearby. (The third primitive, Juan Sisay, is to be found at Santiago Atitlán.)

The afternoon leg of the drive to Quezaltenango passes close to Nahualá, a village five minutes north of the highway and halfway between Katók and Quezaltenango. It also passes through the village of San Cristóbal Totonicapán, from which a rough dirt road winds north up the mountain to San Francisco El Alto (ten minutes) and Momostenango (one hour).

Nahualá is in many ways the most unspoiled of Indian villages; until very recently *ladinos* and the sale of liquor were strictly prohibited. The village is celebrated for its stone *metates* (for grinding corn), its children's toys made of straw and wheat, its black *huipils*, its red-striped belts, its embroidery, its checkered woolen aprons (*rodilleras*) worn by the men. The men's head-shawl (*zut*), blue and embroidered with fantastic figures in yellow and red like showers of sparks, is perhaps the finest single piece of native folk art produced in Guatemala. It is also the most difficult to acquire, since the men who weave and wear it are reluctant to sell—at any price. Market days in Nahualá are Sundays and Thursdays. Fridays in Lent the sacred images are carried to the Stations of the Cross along the crooked streets with the entire population in costume—a sight never to be forgotten. (See Plates 19, 21.)

San Francisco El Alto is perched overlooking the valley at 8661 feet. From the vaulted roof of the ancient colonial church there are two great views. One is of the market (Friday is the day to visit this town) with its wide variety of costumes and dazzlings sunshades (see Plate 10); the other is of the Salamá Valley, with its winding river, golden domes, and distant volcano (Santa María).

Momostenango is better visited on a day's outing from Quezaltenango. The road is not good, and time should be taken to walk down the mountainside from the town to the hot springs, where the famous blankets are washed and the Indians bathe. (See Plate 25.) The festival of Eight Monkey, which takes place annually on an elusively shifting date in the Tzolkín calendar, attracts thousands of pilgrims. At Little Broom and Big Broom, west of the town, the *shimans* (medicine men) officiate by night in front of bonfires built in front of mounds of broken pots—discarded objects returned here to the god who caused them to break.

Quezaltenango, Zuñíl, Champerico

At San Cristóbal Totonicapán there is a crossroads where the highway begins to dip southward through Salcajá to the western capital. Here, at a hot spring tumbling out of the mountainside, an oblong stone basin has been constructed, with bathhouses and cooking sheds behind it. Soapy blue water fills the tub, which doesn't seem to bother thousands of tiny minnows at all. Here come the women of the neighborhood to wash their gorgeous costumes, their babies—and themselves. In the dazzling sunshine, this scene is the undoing of every journeyman painter and photographer.

Jorge Bonifáz, proprietor of Quezaltenango's lordly Pensión Bonifáz, likes to promise his guests guided tours of the various bounties of nature showered upon his neighborhood, but he is wise to let them do their own exploring. Fireworks at night, a drive by Jeep to the active crater of Santiaguito, is an experience. Santiaguito cut loose from the mother volcano, Santa María, at the time (1902) when the latter annihilated virtually everything within artillery range.

Zuñíl, one of the most glorious villages in a country sometimes indifferent to its blessings, has been already described. (Chapter 2, pp. 20–21.) It is a half-hour's drive down the historic pass up which Alvarado dragged his cannon in 1524. Back of the village rises the volcano of the same name. And around Zuñíl Volcano winds a dirt road, higher and higher, narrower and narrower, until it ends in a spot of pure enchantment. Amid the ferns, lianas and orchids of the cliffside there is a sudden rainbow of springs: green (*amarga*), yellow (sulfur), pink (radioactive), silver (cold and fresh), black (of the devil?). This extravaganza of springs is Fuentes Georginas, named in honor of President Jorge Ubico, who commanded a medicinal bath to be built around the emerald-green pool. With its 110° temperature, this is a wonderful place to relax in—if you enter ever so slowly. Here in the clouds a benign "witch" with a crooked stick is the only inhabitant, living in a fire-blackened hut hedged with calla lilies and offering her guests goat cheese and black bread. The air is pure, very cold and soundless.

Beyond Zuñíl the road is paved and meanders southward through vast plantations of cotton, pineapples and rubber. At Retalhuleu one crosses the east-west road (from Tapachula in Mexico to Sonsonate in El Salvador) that parallels the Inter-American. Continuing straight, however, the Zuñíl road comes down to the Pacific at Champerico. There is a fine black-sand beach here, safer than the steeply pitched one at San José, but the town has fallen into decay since the twenties and thirties, when it was a great coffee port. It could become an attractive resort, though better beaches are reputed to lie east along the roadless coast, at Playa Grande and Nueva Venecia.

Backtracking for a moment to conclude one's highland journey, the city of Quezaltenango has a worthy market. It is a block off the main square, and it carries the most extensive stock of eight-foot-long silk *rupas*. These are embroidered belts, an inch to two inches wide, with pompons and trailing streamers of silk thread at the end. Sometimes doubling as a turban, this is one of the more spectacular items of highland costume, and may be seen as far away as Santiago Atitlán. Some say it is woven in Totonicapán, but none were to be found in the market there. No one should leave Guatemala without one.

South to San José and El Salvador

Back in the 1890's Maudslay (see Pp. 6–7), who could rough it with anyone, left Puerto San José in disgust, remarking, "There is not a decent inn in the place." Seventy-five years later there still isn't. The hotels at this dilapidated Pacific resort could only be described by a Faulkner. The lazy electric fans, the walls papered with old newspapers, the rusty iron beds, the rotting wooden floors with cracks wide enough to admit an iguana, contribute to a Deep South atmosphere quite lacking in antebellum romance. Flies, wind and a treacherous undertow are accompaniments to the black-sand beach. This beach, notwithstanding, is wonderful to look at and walk on; but overnight visitors to San José—unless they have friends at Likín, the very posh development with its own swimming pools east of the town—are advised to rent a cottage with cooking facilities at Chulamár.

The Chiquimulilla Canal, which hugs the coast east and west of San José, is also disappointing. In 1943 this waterway was described in Earl Parker Hanson's guide [2] as "vivid with jungle vegetation, red and white herons, egrets, macaws, monkeys, pumas and alligators. The surface of the water is almost covered with the *balon,* a kind of lotus with immaculate white blossoms. The passage of the boat pulls loose masses of the plants with a noise like ripping silk." In 1965 a boat ride through the canal almost to the El Salvador border disclosed nothing more than a family of diminutive gray ducks, two flycatchers and a series of gigantic black anthills in the mangrove roots tangling both banks, nor did all-day trolling in the *balon*-less waters elicit a single strike. The jungles of the Pacific slope have been cut down, and spraying the cotton plantations by plane has apparently eliminated the wildlife that was once so abundant. The thought that a similar fate awaits the tropical wonderlands of the Petén and Lake Izábal to the north should be (but almost certainly isn't) giving the governors of Guatemala nightmares.

The road from the capital to Puerto San José passes through Amatitlán and Escuintla. Enough has been said about *ladino* Escuintla in Chapter 2. Lake Amatitlán has its devotees as a weekend resort. Native middle-class residents of the capital find charms not visible to the naked eye. The waters are choppy and gray. The surrounding mountainous countryside has a moth-eaten look. There is swimming, boating and

[2] *New World Guides to the Latin American Republics,* Vol. 1. Duell, Sloan & Pearce, New York, 1943–5.

fishing of sorts. There is no resort hotel. The village of the same name, twenty-five kilometers from Guatemala City, is *ladino*.

A more attractive place to stop for a swim and a picnic on the way down to San José is the waterfall of San Pedro Martyr, fifty kilometers from the capital and five short of Escuintla. To do this, however, a pass must be obtained from the Empresa Eléctrica de Guatemala in the capital. Turbines near the top of the falls supply most of the power for the region. A walling-up of the gap in the cliff through which the water pours would be required to make this a real tourist attraction, for at present the turbine shed with its tin roof is in plain view. The American company would also have to spend a few dollars digging out the basin, which is presently only two feet deep, and import a little clean sand to cover the rocks, mud and fallen leaves that litter the shore. (Considering the unpopularity of the company with Guatemalan electricity customers, this might be a sound investment.) The hollow cavern, with lianas trailing from the densely wooded rim, is beautiful. The temperature of the water, cool but not cold, is just right.

There are two parallel roads to El Salvador. The southern one, running from Tapachula in Mexico through Retalhuleu and Escuintla, is the fastest and least rewarding. It crosses the eastern border at Pedro de Alvarado and then turns north through Sonsonate to San Salvador. The northern route was not entirely paved in 1965. At that time the drive from the capital to Asunción Mita (149 kilometers) took two hours and fifty minutes. At Asunción Mita the road turns 21 kilometers south to the border, and just short of the border there is a shallow lake, Atescatempa. Here fishermen in their *cayucos* with double-bladed paddles may be seen bringing in sizable hauls of *cilapas*, *tigrillos* and *mojarras* (all of which resemble sunfish). Bathing is good if one doesn't mind wading through water plants to clear water.

Lake Atitlán and Its Villages

Lake Atitlán lies in a deep pocket of the mountains to the south of the Inter-American Highway, about two thirds of the way to Quezaltenango. There is a winding paved road in to it from Patzicía, and a shortcut through Sololá—a southern extension of the road to Chichicastenango that crosses the highway forty-two kilometers beyond the Katók restaurant. Because Sololá, with its superb woolen jackets and bags and its waterfall, is worth visiting, the shortcut is recommended.

Much larger and deeper than Amatitlán, Atitlán has everything that the former lacks: surroundings of spectacular grandeur; a proud Indian population with a wide variety of *trajes* and *costumbres;* plenty of room to move about in. Panajachel, the terminus of both roads connecting the lake to the highway, has hotels and pensions for every taste. It is the natural "base" for trips by boat to the dozen Indian villages surrounding the lake. A launch service operates from the wharf of the Hotel Tzanjuyú.

Panajachel itself is more a cluster of hotels and private week-end residences than a village. The best reason for staying in it—apart from the climate (altitude five thousand feet, as in the capital), the swimming and the view—is its accessibility to the Indian villages. Some of these can be reached by a rocky, dusty road around the eastern rim, but visiting them by boat is more fun. Tzutuhíl and Quiché are the languages spoken in the villages, as they have been since pre-Columbian times.

Santa Catarina is one of two villages within short walking distance of Panajachel. San Jorge is the other. Fishing, crabbing and weaving of *petates* (straw mats) are the principal occupations here. Santa Catarina is in a little cove, its banks thick with the rushes (*tule*) from which the mats are made and a likely place to surprise the *pok*, or Atitlán grebe, a unique flightless bird that is almost extinct, though there is a law against shooting it. The almost perpendicular mountain behind the village is dotted with *milpas*, and amid the yellow corn and occasional blue patch of *anis*, the women in their lovely village costume may be seen working at their stick- or back-looms and at the fountain in front of the church drawing water in earthenware jugs. The church has an elaborate painted façade crowned by rampant lions, black and red on white.

Across the lake to the south, under the three volcanoes for which they are named, are the most famous villages: San Lucas Tolimán, Santiago Atitlán, and San Pedro la Laguna. San Lucas Tolimán, partly because it lies on a north-south trade route and perhaps partly because it is under the sway of the "progressive" Maryknoll Fathers, is half *ladino*-ized. San Pedro la Laguna is a primitive fishing village, its menfolk arrayed in long embroidered trousers, colored shirts and red sashes. Santiago Atitlán, between these two villages, is celebrated for its women's costume: a white *huipil* with purple stripes, an ankle-length red skirt, and a multicolored headband with figures wound round the hair. The women, who are unusually handsome and stride majestically, are worthy of the costume; and so is the village itself as a setting for all this color: streets, walls and huts of black volcanic rock; thatched roofs steeply pitched, smoke pouring out of the peaks. The church dates from 1541. Coffee bushes crowd the slopes behind the village, and directly across the bay are the ruins of Chuitinamit, thought to be the Tzutuhíl capital that Alvarado razed. Here, and at Cerro de Oro on the flank of Tolimán Volcano, buried treasure as well as rich archaeological "beds" are believed to lie, but the villagers are said to regard digging here as sacrilegious and cover up by night what is exposed by day.

All these villages have daily markets and many fiestas. The most interesting of the latter is the Day of the Maximón at Santiago. Every year on Wednesday of Holy Week the image of this Judas is brought out of the house of the *cofrade* assigned to his service. The glass coffin, under a very African crucifixion with grinning skull, is illuminated before the emergence with candlelight. Aromatic yellow-flowering herbs (*Oja de Santa Apolinaria*) hang from the smoky eaves, mingled with red gourdes, large balls of paper trash in nets, and sausages. Pine needles cover the black stone floor on which the yellow tapers flicker.

Dressed, like every other male in Santiago, in mauve striped pants, but sporting a shiny new pair of *ladino* shoes, three felt hats and a foot-long cigar, the Maximón emerges from the *cofrade*'s house promptly at 1 P.M. Asked what the Maximón signified, the *cofrade* answered: "Alvarado. He's a bad spirit, but he can do good if you treat him properly." Amid the funeral wail of sax and trumpet and a steady roll of drums, the Maximón is borne rapidly through the streets to the Municipal Building—"to intercede for our difficulties with the government," the *cofrade* confided. First he is set up facing the church, while the thirty bearers who accompany him decorate the altars with flowers and fruit. Then he is placed in a small outside Moorish-style chapel, built for him some years ago when a padre refused him the church—and was almost killed for refusing. There he is tied with ropes to a straight pole, where he remains until Good Friday, when he is returned to his "grave" in the *cofrade*'s attic to join all the old Maximóns. The Indians' ambiguous attitude toward this Alvarado-figure is perhaps best demonstrated by the fact that in 1965 two Indians were observed attaching a Turkish towel with safety pins to the Maximón's neck to protect him from the cold night air.

Huehuetenango, Chichicastenango, the Northwest

North of Atitlán two north-south roads bisect the northwestern highlands, parallel to each other. The westernmost is the Inter-American Highway itself, passing through Huehuetenango in a more westerly direction through the gorge known as El Tapón (The Plug) to the Mexican border, and from there on to Comitán, San Cristóbal de las Casas, Oaxaca and Mexico City. Motorists entering Guatemala by this route—which is recommended because of its greater scenic and historic interest over the southern one via Tapachula—are nevertheless warned that El Tapón in rainy seasons is hazardous with landslides and sometimes impassable. The highway's engineers selected an unstable valley, and there seems to be no way of keeping the paved part of the road paved. The Tapachula route, in contrast, is level, paved, and fast.

As the highway begins to turn north to Huehuetenango at the San Cristóbal crossroads, there is the branch road (dirt) to San Francisco El Alto and Momostenango already mentioned. Huehuetenango, with its little Hotel Zaculeu, is a good place to stay a day or a week; a day if the object is only to savor the town and the nearby ruins of Zaculeu (see Chapter 1, p. 11), a week if the traveler desires to penetrate the Indian country to the north. There is daily service by four-wheel-drive bus to Todos Santos Chuchumatán and some of the isolated Indian settlements farther north. Todos Santos is the village made famous by Maud Oakes.[3] Its altitude is 8200 feet and the pass leading to it (The Windy Place) is 3000 feet higher still. La Farge tells of a mail carrier frozen to death in this pass in April. Maud Oakes describes unforgettably the apple and peach orchards sprawling over the walls, the nearby Maya ruins, the savage rooster race that still takes place on the day following All Saints' Day, the wisdom of the prayermakers and *shimans* and the suppressed (but occasionally violent) antagonism between the Indians and their *ladino* exploiters. ("Señorita, when you asked Simona to eat with you, it made us *naturales* curious, for a *ladino* would never do that. It changed our feelings for you.")

The road to Chichicastenango crosses the Inter-American Highway a few miles north of Sololá and continues (north of Chichi) to Santa Cruz del Quiché and finally to Sacapulas, where it intersects the east-west road running from Cobán to Huehuetenango. Chichicastenango is the most famous of the all-Indian villages. Tourists overrun it, but they have had remarkably little effect on the intense Christo-pagan rites practiced in the two facing churches and none at all on the brilliant craftsmanship of the woolweavers and embroiderers. For those who do not like to see Christianity and paganism happily mixed, the strictly pagan rites at the stone *ídolo* called Pascual Abáj across one of the *barrancos* are worth visiting. Here chickens are sacrificed to the Maya

---

[3] *Beyond the Windy Place*, Farrar, Straus & Co., New York, 1951. A study in depth of the same village, *Two Crosses of Todos Santos*, was published in the same year by the same author. Twenty years earlier Oliver La Farge and Douglas Byers had made a somewhat similar study of nearby Jacaltenango, *The Year Bearer's People*, Middle American Research Institute of Tulane University, New Orleans, La., 1931.

deity, and at the bottom of the *barranco* is a little "factory" where the Alvarado masks are made for the Dance of the Conquest. This is a long walk, and the walk to a swimming pool in an even deeper gorge to the right of the Quiché road is more arduous; but both are worth the time and exertion. (See Plates 15, 16, 17.)

According to Brasseur de Bourbourg, *Chichicastenango* is a word in the Nahuatl tongue meaning "place of the bramble bushes." Its people call themselves Maxeños, after the last syllable of their patron saint's name. Santo Tomás Chichicastenango (to give it its full name) is neither the purest nor the most typical of the Indian villages, but it is the wealthiest (investment in the tourist trade demands that it be not spoiled) and the one most likely to be visited by the average traveler. Nestling in the piny mountains at seven thousand feet, its climate is cold and often foggy. Its costumes of black wool embroidered with red and purple braid [4] and its sprawling white plaster houses with red tiled roofs dominated by two massive colonial churches facing each other across the plaza make it the most picturesque of "stage-sets" imaginable. Even on ordinary market days (Sundays, Thurdays) Chichi is something to see. But during the big fiestas (St. Thomas', December 18–21; Holy Week; All Saints', November 1) the village becomes as kaleidoscopic with color, as overcrowded, as boisterous and drunken as a Brueghel painting. A strange *quietness*, withal, gives to this reeling about amid clouds of copal incense a pervasive air of mystery; for the Indian is never on parade, never seemingly aware that he is being watched, never shaken out of his subconscious subservience to the conquering race, whose victory he celebrates in pantomime, almost in slow motion, as if to exorcise his suffering with his humiliation.

On the final day of the festival of the town's patron saint, images from all the surrounding villages are carried through the streets and mingle with those of the fourteen *cofradías*. At the climactic moment, those of Saint Thomas, Saint Joseph and Saint Sebastian, on red-canopied daises flashing with tiny mirrors, come down the crowded steps of the main church, mingle with the other saints, and return to the three portals. Then the *Tzijolach*, a tiny horse and rider symbolizing Santiago, the Conquerors' patron saint, is pulled up and down a rope attached to the belfry, never quite reaching heaven or earth. Whatever else he symbolizes, *Tzijolach* is the special mascot of the rocket bearers, for with his appearance their activity, already thunderous during the

---

[4] Chichicastenango is one of the few Indian towns where *both* men and women still wear the traditional *trajes* (costumes). The men's was copied from a Spanish military outfit of the sixteenth century.

preceding days and nights, redoubles. The dancers in their red wigs and Alvarado-masks mount their hobbyhorses and have a last fling. The Quiché and Cakchiquel chiefs prepare to relose the ultimate battle. The babies are taken to be christened. The flying *voladores* come down from their pole. The marimbas that have been playing the secular dance *El Son* in the adjacent *cantinas* are wheeled indoors. The *shimans* at the *quemadores* on the steps of the two churches stop swinging their censers. The copal smoke and the acrid odor of gunpowder subside. The last of the reeling *Maxeños* is gently dragged home by his dutiful wife. The few real troublemakers are in jail. By dawn, those sober enough to make it are on their way to work in the mountains. And Chichicastenango is again a *ladino* town—until next market day.

Padre Rossbach (see Chapter 3, p. 34) has a worthy successor as parish priest of Chichi in Padre Casas. He is said to have "converted" seven thousand Indians, but he supports the all-Indian school and denounces the *ladinos* quite openly for their immorality and material- ism, pointing out, for example, in a 1965 sermon, that only two of them had bothered to show up for Mass on their own Saints' days. He frowns on the pagan *costumbres* but doesn't interfere with the activi- ties of the powerful *cofradías*. He insists only that candles be placed in a long gutter down the center of the nave rather than all over the church floor and that drunks remain outside the two buildings.

Santa Cruz del Quiché, the capital of the province, is an hour's drive north of Chichi on Route 15—an hour if time is included for the short run out of this town to Utatlán (see Chapter 2, p. 22), the Quiché capital Alvarado leveled. A half hour farther north is San Pedro Joco- pilas, an attractive town with a commanding view of a white graveyard to its west. Each hamlet from here on is beautiful and untouched by commercialism, the houses spotlessly white or Tamayo-blue, under gently sloping tiled roofs with umber woodwork.

Sacapulas, at the end of the road and four hours' leisurely driving from Chichi, is celebrated for its salt beds and its *alfenique,* a pulled molasses candy. At the approach to the town, women may be seen winding the candy around wall hooks or stretching it between trees; the finished "cakes" receive their pattern from the straw *petates* on which they are laid out to dry in the sun. Less celebrated, but un- deservedly, is the interior of Sacapulas' church. Its soot-black square piers and its dozens of splendidly carved wooden saints and angels just dusty enough to scintillate in the shafts of sunlight entering through cracks in the doors, contribute to a devotional atmosphere the cata- combs must have had. The outstanding image is a black-robed Christ in a glass case, so flyspecked and cobwebbed that nothing can be distinguished but the highlights on the gaunt face and the orange flowers held in one hand.

At Sacapulas the road north comes to an end, and one may turn left to Huehuetenango or right to Cobán; but above the town, on a branch road just before Cuñén, there is a cluster of villages—Nebáj, Cotzál, Chajúl—that this author has never visited. All of them are said to be rich in ruins and in unusual costumes. Near Chajúl a cataract of water bursts from the solid rock to form one of the sources of the Chixoy, a river that joins the Pasión at Altar de Sacrificios to form the mighty Usumacinta, dividing Guatemala from Mexico.

Cobán and Its Environs

One way, and perhaps the pleasantest, of getting to Cobán, is to continue eastward past Cuñén on the road just described. Another is to climb directly up from the capital, by way of San Juan Sacatepéquez, Rabinal and Salamá; this is a long way on a bad road. Only slightly easier is the "usual" way of driving to Cobán, cutting north off the Atlantic Highway at El Rancho to Salamá. There are other ways, all complicated, all interesting. Flying to Cobán—if the clouds there ever lift enough to permit a landing—is the least interesting.

Cobán has a very special aura, difficult to describe. San Pedro Carchá, only eighteen kilometers north of Cobán, is the second biggest *municipio* in Guatemala, but no connoisseur of cities has ever been known to stay there or to talk about it after passing through. Not that Cobán is beautiful to look at—its buildings are nondescript, and its central bandstand (known locally as The Tortilla Smasher) rivals the one in Costa Rica's capital as the ugliest structure in Central America. But an almost tangible nostalgia for great days gone hangs over the town, and its setting and surroundings have a hypnotic effect. The German coffee merchants, whatever else they did, brought order, cleanliness and prosperity to Cobán, and from their expulsion in 1944 the town has never quite recovered. Climbing the steps to the Calvario, from which a stunning view of the whole valley unfolds (Plate 24), Cobán lies tucked in its fragrant hills and clouds like a melancholy memory of grandeur, a moment arrested in time, a promise still waiting to be fulfilled.

No one has ever accused the Germans of having done anything reprehensible to Guatemala, but what made them so unconscious of evil in their homeland and so foolish is a mystery. Doña Lulú Hempstead, owner of the Posada inn and matriach of Cobán, whose father was the first German to settle here (1864) but whose mother was English and educated her to despise authoritarianism, shakes her head over the pity of it. "They seemed to see no inconsistency," she says, "in intermarrying with the Indians and yet accepting Hitler's lunacy about a Pure Nordic Race. They were captivated by his idea of eating from a single pot on Sundays. They said it was so cozy! They approved of his idea of having big families, of course, and when they returned from visits to the Fatherland in the thirties they would go into sentimental ecstasies about the Discipline and the Enthusiasm and the Oneness of it all." The expulsion of the Germans coincided with the fall of Ubico. "Almost the last heritage of Las Casas' time was the great clock tower. The *ladinos* with their idea of progress decided it must go." Doña Lulú laughed bitterly. "It took them almost six months to tear it down! General Ubico would never have permitted it. He loved Cobán. Even the Habsburg Double-Eagle of Charles V was torn off San Pedro's church. Why? No reason. They just can't wait to reduce the beauty of the past, the countryside, and the Indian, to their level."

In the countryside round about Cobán little changes. The Kekchi and Pokomán women are still arrayed like queens. Driving along the Polochíc River between Tamahú and Tucurú, high mountains wreathed in mist loom over both sides of the narrow valley, their flanks glistening with the different greens of banana and castor bean, pine and giant fern. Orchids hang from the *ceibas*, brandishing their red daggers. Yellow-flowering *chacté* and red-flowering *chiltoté* seem but earthly extensions of the birds that fly between them, *montezumas* and gold-black Guatemalan orioles. The women in their blue skirts and wine-dark *huipils* carry bundles of daisies on their heads, their necks supporting "breast-plates" of Peruvian silver coin. Through caverns hung with lianas the rushing river flows, now filling deep pools, now crashing into boulders and sending white spray as high as the road. The stones of the crumbling churches are covered with an orange lichen so brilliant that the walls seem to tremble in the sun. And on the verandas of the thatched huts from which smoke rises to mingle with the clouds hang pyramids of yellow tapers suspended by their wicks. Only the men, with their long machetes in leathern scabbards, bent over under the immense packs hung from the tumplines across their foreheads, seem out of key with this efflorescence, living reminders of the centuries of subjugation.

San Cristóbal Verapáz with its legendary lake, Lanquín and Cahabón with their caves, San Juan Chamelco with its famous bell and silver, San Pedro Carchá with its pottery and deliciously cold reservoir, Tactíc with its church full of polychrome sculpture—these, and other surrounding villages still to be "discovered," are the glory of Cobán. These and the landscape, the people, the melancholy, and the mystery.

Lake Izabál, Livingston, Puerto Barrios

As so often in travel, the hard way of getting to these ornaments of Guatemala's Caribbean lowland is the best way. In this instance, via Cobán. There is a launch leaving the western end of Lake Izabál every Thursday at dawn. If arrangements are made in advance in the capital, the launch will tow a car-carrying iron barge behind it. The point of embarkation is El Estór (The Store). El Estór is a pleasant day's drive from Cobán. Thinking in terms of a week's excursion from the capital, then—a sort of Great Circle Route of Guatemala's Middle Wonderland—it is possible to leave the capital early of a Sunday morning and take either of the following two suggested itineraries:

	I	II
Sunday Night	Chichicastenango	Huehuetenango
Monday Night	Cobán	Cobán
Tuesday Night	Cobán	Cobán
Wednesday Night	El Estór	El Estór
Thursday Night	Livingston	Livingston
Friday Night	Barrios	Barrios
Saturday Night	Guatemala City	Guatemala City

The alternate itinerary (II) is suggested for those travelers who have already visited Chichi and would prefer to spend a day exploring the remote Indian villages—Nebáj, Cotzál, Chajúl—mentioned on P. 117. This would involve spending the first night at Huehuetenango's Hotel Zaculeu with time enough after the drive to inspect the ruins of the same name. Monday, after a very early morning start from Huehue, could be spent visiting the Indian villages and driving on to Cobán. All of Tuesday would be spent in and around Cobán, having an afternoon swim in San Cristóbal's lake, and returning in time to see the city by sunset from the Calvario. The remainder of the trip would follow the schedule of Itinerary I, now to be described.

The reader has already been briefed on the road to Chichi, the sights of that town and the comforts of its Mayan Inn, the road north to Cobán via Sacapulas, Cobán itself. From Cobán to El Estór the road is dirt, and adequate all the way. The churches at Tactíc, Tamahú and Tucurú may be visited during the morning leg of the drive. Tucurú (Kekchi for "Owl") has a restaurant that serves a good lunch. Most of the afternoon part of the drive parallels the *Ferrocarril Verapáz*, a remarkable railway that begins and ends nowhere. It "begins" at Pancajché, where the grade on up to Cobán proved unmanageable, and it "ends" at Panzós, where Cobán's coffee could then be reloaded onto barges in the Polochíc River for the rest of the journey via Lake Izabál to the sea. When the automobile road was opened up after the war, it became cheaper to transport the coffee to El Estór by truck. But the railroad still operates! Asked why, an engineer shrugged his shoulders expressively and said: "Who knows? *Costumbre* [habit]. If we stopped running it, we'd forget how...."

There is a tiny hotel at the lake port of El Estór run by Felipe Bautista. It is clean and the food is good. The proprietor is very accommodating about waking his guests up by flashlight Thursdays in time to make the dawn departure of *La Liberación*. But it is advisable to arrive at El Estór before dark Wednesday night in order to drive one's car onto the iron barge and get it lashed down. The trip through the lake and the Rio Dulce begins whenever the crew wakes up and decides to leave. Arrangements should be made to stop for a swim and an inspection of the restored San Felipe Castle (see Chapter 5, p. 72) en route. The *Liberación* next passes Cayo Palomo, a jungle island that had been "leased" in 1963 by Bill Taft, a professional hunter and fisherman from San Francisco. There he had built a lodge for visitors. But if arrangements are made in advance to extend the trip and stay with Taft for hunting and fishing, his island should be reached from Livingston *after* one's car has been unloaded there, pending the final leg by boat to Barrios.

Lake Izabál, unless one is lucky enough to see a manatee or has time to fish the inlets and river at the western end, is dull and gray. But the passage of the Golfete, and the Río Dulce into which it narrows, is beautiful—and sometimes exciting. Waves break over the barge. The water becomes clear, very deep, and blue. Leaping fish may be seen. Jungle comes down to the shoreline. The white cliffs in the narrow stretch of the outlet are almost perpendicular and fifty to a hundred feet high. Livingston is situated on a palm-shaded promontory at the mouth of the Río Dulce.

Ludwig Anker's Del Mar Hotel is the place to spend the night in Livingston. The town is utterly unlike any other in Guatemala. Its people are variously described as Caribs, Black Caribs or Negroes. Whatever they are, they are neither Indian nor *ladino*, and like the people of Belize up the coast whom they resemble, they are more given to laughter and gay night-life than typical Guatemalans. There were Caribs already settled on the Honduras coast to the south of here when Columbus landed. Negro slaves from the Bay Islands, brought thither from the Leewards by the British in the eighteenth century, escaped to the mainland. The races mingled and began to move up and down the coast. Livingston's population is one happy result of that migration. It guards its heritage. Manioc (cassava) is the staple food, not corn. As in Haiti, each man is apt to take to himself several "wives" and settle each in a separate house—as far away from each other as possible, naturally. The repertoire of songs and dances, some going back to the original Carib homeland in Paraguay, is extensive.

From Livingston, Puerto Barrios can be reached *only* by boat. The *Liberación* continues on; the local office of the Ferrocarril Verapáz provides other ferries. Barrios' working population is more Negro than Carib, and as a town it is less exotic, dirtier, and noisier with the backwash of the banana and shipping trades than Livingston. There are probably more jukeboxes, slot machines, bars, and whorehouses here than even in Escuintla; but the atmosphere is less depressing. Sailors from all over the world give it a cosmopolitan timbre. The Hotel Del Norte, within a block of United Fruit's slatternly headquarters, has good seafood and a certain gaslight charm. The place to swim is the tree-shaded public pool at Puerto Matías de Galvéz, a more modern and tasteful harbor the government is developing to the south of the bay.

Quiriguá

The Atlantic Highway has already been mentioned. It parallels Guatemala's biggest river, the Motagua, almost as far as El Rancho and then cuts through the mountains in a southwesterly direction to the capital. The great pre-Columbian ruins at Quiriguá (see Chapter 1, p. 10) are one hundred kilometers from Puerto Barrios and they are the major point of interest on the six-hour drive back to Guatemala City. Although the site is only a few hundred yards from the speedway, it is not easy to get to—or even to find. A Coca-Cola sign on a high bluff southeast of the highway bears the name of the place in very small type. From there a dirt road leads to the United Fruit Company's banana railway paralleling the highway. It was in 1910, when the jungles were being cut down, that Victor Cutter of United Fruit set aside seventy-five acres of mahogany and *ceiba* surrounding the ruins, as a reservation in perpetuity. In its palmier days, United Fruit carried visitors to the ruins by rail. Now there is a forty-minute walk along the ties in the hot sun. If one turns *left* at the tracks, one will reach the ruins. How worthwhile this effort is may be indicated by Morley's tribute: "I have visited Quiriguá on nine occasions; indeed I never lose an opportunity of stopping off there when in Guatemala, to renew my friendship with the monuments."

The place to stop for lunch, after visiting Quiriguá, is the Posada Doña María to the right of the highway at Kilometer Marker 180. The Río Doña María has been dammed up and there is a turquoise pool right behind the restaurant that is wonderful to dive and swim in. Another good swimming hole is at the foot of a twenty-foot falls at a place called Pasa Bien, also north of the highway and about halfway between Barrios and Guatemala City. To the south of the highway near here is the road leading to Zacapa, Chiquimula and the shrine of the Black Christ at Esquipulas; from this road a left fork leads to the Honduras border and Copán.

Esquipulas

It is not feasible to visit Esquipulas or Copán on the way to or from anything. They must be ends in themselves, for the roads are not good. Until the roads are improved, the best way to get to Esquipulas is by plane (Aviateca) and the time to go there is January 15 (Esquipulas Day) or during Lent or Holy Week. Penitents from all over Central America make this the most overcrowded shrine on the continent save Mexico's Tepeyac (see Plate 23). Copán (see Chapter 1, p. 9) is most easily reached by plane or car from San Pedro Sula in Honduras; visitors who want to make it from Guatemala are advised to leave their cars at Vado Hondo (south of Chiquimula) and take the Jeep service from there to the border. There are good pensions at Chiquimula and a small but pleasant inn at Copán. In the rainy season this excursion is impossible.

Returning to the Atlantic Highway, there are several colonial churches just off the road on the final stretch to the capital. San Cristóbal Acasaguastlan and San Agustin Acasaguastlan, on opposite sides of the highway halfway between Zacapa and El Rancho, are the finest of these. Both have arched stone roofs and quadrangular earthquake-proof towers like the massive shrine at Esquipulas. San Cristóbal has a good collection of painted stone saints and a handsome goldleaf altar.

The Petén and Belize

There is no way of telling a traveler how to get to the Petén or what to do when he gets there. There is no all-weather road into the huge territory. There are airstrips, but most of them, even where famous Maya ruins show on the map, are just freight-drops. Except for the standard flight to Tikál there are no regularly scheduled excursions. The Jungle Lodge at Tikál is the only thing approaching a hotel in the territory, though its enterprising proprietor, Tono Ortíz, is developing similar rustic facilities at Sayaxché and Tayasál (Flores). Ortíz, Clark Tours, Joya Hairs-Susan Miles (*Sakbé Safaris*), and others, organize fancy pack trips into the wilds from time to time, complete with sleeping bags, outdoor showers, dugouts-with-outboards, carbide lamps, fishing tackle, rifles and various mating calls for the diffident *tigre*.

No attempt will be made here to cover sights (and sites) in the Petén exhaustively. A team of explorers, mapmakers and archaeologists would have to crisscross the jungle systematically for a year; then they would have to be followed by roadbuilders and airstrip engineers—and let's hope this never happens. For the attraction of the Petén is in never knowing quite where you are or what you may find. There is a project to build an all-weather road north from the Atlantic Highway near Bananera, bridge the outlet to Lake Izabál at the San Felipe Fort and then connect with the existing trail from Puerto Modesto Mendez on the Sarstoon to Flores, the island capital of the Petén in Lake Petén-Itzá. From Flores there is a trail, viable to four-wheel-drive vehicles, east to the Belize border at Benque Viejo, from which a paved road (with bus service) continues on to Belize City. The only other road that even approaches the Petén is the one north from Cobán to Seból. This road was drivable in 1965, but its 107 kilometers constituted an all-day trip in a rugged vehicle. Near Lanquín a tributary of the Chixoy River may be picked up and (if there has been enough rain to swell it) followed by canoe all the way to its junction with the Pasión at Altar de Sacrificios. At Seból is the Río Seból, southernmost extension of the Pasión, and navigable all the way north to the same junction, past the important ruins of El Seibál (presently being excavated by a team of archaeologists from Harvard), and past Sayaxché, with its airstrip, lodges, and good road to Flores, two hours' drive north. The road to Seból through Kekchi country is very beautiful: orchids, air plants and cloud forest before descending through jungle to the teal-blue river.

In between the two rivers (the Chixoy and the Seból-Pasión) is an inexhaustible wonderland of fauna and flora, the "corner" of the Petén that is most accessible. If not reached by canoe from either of the rivers, the easier way is to fly to Sayaxché and rent a dugout with an outboard motor (and a guide). The largest of the many lakes in this region is the Petexbatún. Like all of them, it is surrounded by climax forest, alive with animals and fish. A little river leads south to it from the Pasión, and other little rivers connect with smaller lakes. One of these streams (one of many) may be pursued to its source. Following the bends over ledges of intricately bowled and fluted limestone, with water lilies choking the margin and even seeming to flower under water, one comes finally to a circular pool. It is perhaps thirty feet deep and fifty feet in diameter. The bottom is sandy, but here and there clusters of broken fresh-water mollusk shells of the deepest imaginable blue are flecked with tiny spots of scarlet. Around these sand patches are underwater plants, their yellow-green leaves undulating rhythmically as the water bubbles up from the bottom. Thousands of tiny, iridescent fish with yellow eyes swim in and out of this submarine garden.

If it seems almost sacrilegious to fish in such a virgin paradise, the determined sportsman is advised to continue north to Flores and arrange for an Aviateca flight to Melchor de Mencos. Five minutes across the border at Benque Viejo he will have no trouble picking up a bus to Belize (see Chapter 5, p. 68), and at Belize hunting and fishing are organized by professionals who leave nothing to chance. Two of these, Emmet Gowan of Tennessee and Vic Barothy of Michigan, Key West, and Cuba, fly most of their customers in directly from New Orleans, Chicago or New York. Barothy has lodges both on the Belize River and on the offshore keys: tarpon, snook, and big-game hunting from the river lodge; bone, marlin, kingfish, and spearfishing for red snappers and angels from the island camps. There is a special for big game hunters: "$1,500 for ten days, a jaguar guaranteed, or your money back."

If not lodging with the fishermen, the places to stay at Belize are the Fort George Hotel (with pool) or the more modest but comfortable Bellevue, presided over by Miss Jean Dinger.

INDEX

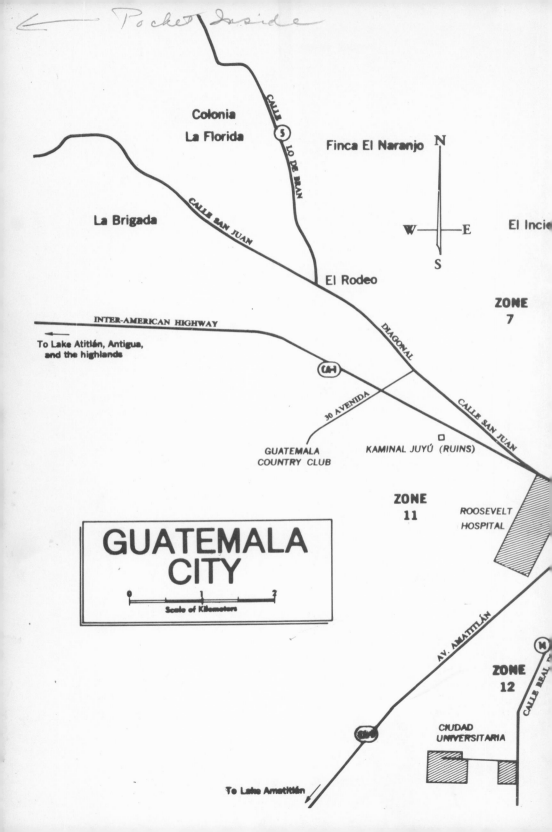

Pocket Inside

Colonia
La Florida

CALLE LO DE BRAN

5

Finca El Naranjo

N

W ── E

S

CALLE SAN JUAN

La Brigada

El Rodeo

El Incie

ZONE
7

INTER-AMERICAN HIGHWAY

To Lake Atitlán, Antigua,
and the highlands

DIAGONAL

CA

30 AVENIDA

CALLE SAN JUAN

GUATEMALA
COUNTRY CLUB

KAMINAL JUYÚ (RUINS)

ZONE
11

ROOSEVELT
HOSPITAL

GUATEMALA
CITY

0   1   2
Scale of Kilometers

AV. AMATITLÁN

CALLE REAL

ZONE
12

CIUDAD
UNIVERSITARIA

To Lake Amatitlán